FRESWATER AQUARIUM

The complete guide
to setting up the aquarium of your dreams

ISBN : 9798868057496

Copyright © by AquaHealth, 2023
All rights reserved

No part of this book may be reproduced or transformed in any form or by any means, graphic, electronic or mechanical, including photocopying, recording, taping or by any information storage retrieval system, without the written permission of the author.

Who are we ?

At AquaHealth we've been passionate about aquariums since we were very young. Through our various books on aquaristics and the maintenance of fish and invertebrates of all species in aquariums, we hope to transmit our knowledge of this passion which has driven us for so many years.

In this way, we hope to enable as many people as possible, young and old alike, to discover, appreciate and become passionate about this fascinating world of aquaristics, as we have done !

To know Mother Nature, is to love her smallest creation.

Takashi Amano

CONTENTS

FIRST STEPS

- 8 An aquarium : why and for whom?
- 9 Reconstructing a piece of nature
- 10 Science above all

BRINGING AN AQUARIUM TO LIFE

- 12 The basics of aquarium keeping
- 14 The budget
- 15 Technique and equipment
- 29 (Plants)
- 33 The water
- 45 The nitrogen cycle
- 51 Set up your first aquarium
- 62 Aquarium care
- 67 Feeding your fish

COMMON PROBLEMS AND SOLUTIONS

- 72 Water parameters problems
- 72 (Algae)
- 78 Diseases
- 81 Change an element in the aquarium

THE DIFFERENT TYPES OF AQUARIUM

- 84 Which aquarium to choose?
- 85 The community aquarium
- 90 The specific aquarium
- 91 The nano-aquarium
- 93 The biotope aquarium
- 95 Aquascaping

THE SHEETS

- 102 Fish sheets
- 118 Plant sheets
- 130 Disease sheets

FIRST STEPS

An aquarium : why and for whom ?

Aquarium keeping consists of raising aquatic animals in an aquarium : a tank with transparent sides allow observation and in which plants and animals are kept and displayed. This is the literal definition. I would personally define aquarium keeping as above all a passion or at least, a strong interest, with objective of recreating an authentic ecosystem, pleasant to those who contemplate it and adapted to the needs of the living beings who occupy it. And it is based on this definition that we will approach aquarium keeping throughout this book.

Why install an aquarium?

Whether it is to observe and understand a real natural aquatic world, to empower your children, to create an elegant and unique decorative work for a room in the house or to acquire a particular aquatic species that you have had a crush on, there is no shortage of reasons. It has also now been demonstrated through numerous scientific studies that an aquarium provides numerous health benefits, particularly in reducing daily stress. Observing this piece of nature recreated in a corner of your living room, office, or bedroom can literally relax you and help to reduce stress-related illnesses. So the real question to ask yourself is not why install an aquarium, but why have you still not installed one (or even several!) ?

However, before rushing to the first pet store, you must keep in mind the constraints imposed by an aquarium (if you want to do things right) which we're going to discover right now.

For whom ?

Let us always keep in mind that an aquarium involves lives, with animals having a form of consciousness, sensitivity and being able to live for several years or even decades in the case of some fish species.

▲ What child has never been amazed in an aquarium shop ?

If you buy an aquarium for your child, they may lose interest more or less quickly. It is therefore absolutely necessary to ask yourself a few questions beforehand to be sure of your choice and your future responsibility. For example, ask yourself who will take care of the aquarium and their ability to devote a minimum hour of their time each week to maintenance. Or ask yourself if you can relocate him/her if your situation requires it ? How to organize absences ? So many important questions whose full extent we do not necessarily understand when we start. Fortunately, throughout this book we will see all these elements to take into account to get a clear idea of what awaits you !

FIRST STEPS

Reconstruct a piece of nature

To be adapted to the life that will evolve there, your aquarium should ideally recreate a piece of nature in its own right. With this in mind, it must only contain natural elements and respect certain major biochemical principles. The goal is to recreate and maintain a true miniature ecosystem. Let's take advantage of this part to immediately start on a good basis and see what will (and will not) be necessary to do to achieve this!

First, avoid as much as possible the "advice" of pet store salespeople, who are rarely reliable and wise. There is no question here of denigrating or generalizing (I myself have already met some truly passionate sellers and very qualified in aquariums) but, let's admit, this remains rather rare, with the main objective remaining for all the same : sell.
And beginners represent perfect predilection targets for quickly purchasing animals and products that are poorly suited/unnecessary to customer needs and very often with little consideration for animal welfare.

Before any purchase (animals or equipment), take the time to obtain information from various sources and mature your project. But if you are reading this book, it is because you have already integrated this approach and for that, I already congratulate you !

Secondly, you will have to demonstrate an essential quality, to be acquired by any aquarist : **patience**.
Nature and life are the result of incredible scientific feats, functioning in a balance as formidable in its efficiency as in its fragility. And for all of this to come to fruition, the Earth needed time. A lot of time !
I assure you, to create our own aquatic world, it will not take us several billion years. Nature and its study have already given us a good model to follow and replicate. However, to establish and maintain this balance within our creation, it will be essential not to rush things by wanting to skip steps.

FIRST STEPS

Science above all

Like the nature that surrounds us, the world artificially recreated within an aquarium operates based on a certain number of principles. Thus, without being a precise science, aquarium science involves numerous scientific fields : chemistry for the composition of water, physics for fluid dynamics and thermal exchanges, biology and biochemistry for the interaction between plants, fish and their environment, electricity or even home automation for the (almost) autonomous operation of the aquarium and even mathematics for the calculation of the different volumes... This omnipresent part of science can discourage or disorient when you are starting out, due to the complexity that it can appear. But don't panic ! By taking the time to properly inform yourself about the different key points as proposed in this book, you will see that it is not necessary to obtain a Nobel Prize in science to maintain a healthy aquarium.

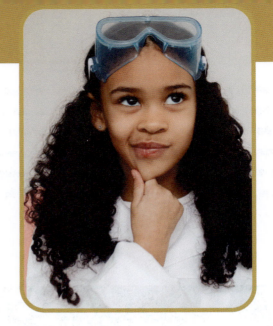

Exercise n°1 : Applied mathematics

To prove that aquarium keeping is simpler than it seems, let's do a first math exercise. If just reading the name of this subject makes you feel a breakout and horrible school memories, don't worry, these will be the only ones in the book that we will write !

We need math (it works better when we abbreviate their name) to calculate an elementary data in aquariums : the tank volume. Indeed, it is from this mesure that a certain number of important elements will arise, such as the type and quantity of fish that you can put in your aquarium. for example.

And to calculate it, nothing could be simpler. Just multiply the length of the tank (l), by its width (w) and finally by its height (h) (values in cm or inch), then divide the result by 1000 if mesures are in cm or by 231 if in inch. We obtain, with this aquarium :

$$\text{Volume} = (120 \times 40 \times 50) / 1000$$
$$= 240{,}000 / 1000 = 240 \text{ liters}$$

or

$$\text{Volume} = (47{,}2 \times 15{,}7 \times 19{,}7) / 231$$
$$= 14\,599 / 231 = 63 \text{ gal}$$

Simple, right ?

BRINGING AN AQUARIUM TO LIFE

BRING AN AQUARIUM TO LIFE

The basics of aquarium keeping

When you start, the word aquarium hobby has very little meaning, or even a rather reductive meaning, suggesting that it is only a matter of a few fish held between five panes of glass.
Aquarium keeping is in reality a complex, time-consuming and potentially expensive activity, but exciting and satisfying when done correctly. Let's see what these consist of and above all how to best get started.

Anticipate and prepare your project

These may seem like big words if you just want to acquire a small (or large) aquarium without pretension, but you must nevertheless go through this key step. This will indeed be decisive in the success of your first experience and in the pleasure you will derive from it.

The first thing will be to think before any purchase about the type of fish or invertebrates you would like to acquire. Depending on this choice and the specific needs of the species(s) selected, you will be able to adapt the necessary equipment accordingly and then see the feasibility of the project based on other constraints. It is always simpler and less frustrating to think along these lines. Imagine otherwise the disappointment of realizing that the aquarium you bought without really knowing what you would put in it at that moment, is ultimately too small or unsuitable for the fish you fell for...

Obviously, in addition to your personal desires, you will have to take into account other constraints :

- The location available in your home to place the aquarium
- A support to place it on (or to provide)
- Your budget
- Possibly an adapted home insurance (in case of aquariums with large volumes)

The size of your aquarium will therefore be determined by all of these factors. But it is the size criterion that will subsequently influence everything else :

- The choice of the species of fish(es) (if your initial choice cannot be made because of an aquarium size that you cannot afford) and the total number of individuals
- Ease of maintenance
- The complexity of creating and maintaining the aquarium viable

Despite what you may believe, "large" aquariums are not the most difficult to start with. On the contrary, they are easier to keep stable and less dangerous for fish than small (nano) aquariums, which are much more sensitive.
A volume of 20 to 30 us gal (80 to 120 liters) is a good compromise when starting out.

The basics of aquarium keeping

The support

It is imperative to always hold a clear notion of the precise weight of your future aquarium in order to adequately dimension its support. For instance, a 26 us gal (100 liters) aquarium can weigh anywhere between 150 and 200 kilograms, while a 80 us gal (300 liters) aquarium may even reach up to 500 kilograms ! Therefore, it is essential to properly size the support so that it proves sufficiently robust and steadfast, not to yield under this load over time. It should also exhibit flawless stability, with an even distribution of weight on the floor and a perfectly level orientation (to be verified using a spirit level for example). Please note that you should never place an aquarium on a mobile support, such as a rolling table.

You have several options for addressing this requirement. You can consider purchasing a purpose-built aquarium stand, ensuring that it meets the aforementioned criteria. Alternatively, you may use an existing piece of furniture, but make sure it complies with the specified conditions. Lastly, you have the option to construct your own support structure using wooden battens or metal rails, which can be either screwed or welded into place.

Location of the aquarium

The choice of the location is of paramount importance. As mentioned, once filled, an aquarium can bear a considerable weight that is challenging to move without draining it. Consequently, it is vital to be absolutely certain of your decision. To determine the optimal position, you should :

- Avoid proximity to heat sources such as radiators, ovens, or direct sunlight to prevent excessive water temperature fluctuations.
- Ensure that there is a nearby water source for convenient maintenance.
- Establish a safe environment around the aquarium with easy access.
- Ensure an adequate number of electrical outlets, ideally positioned above the aquarium.
- Refrain from locating the aquarium in certain rooms like the kitchen or bathroom due to potentially toxic emissions for aquatic life (e.g., grease vapors, cosmetics) or in high-traffic areas such as a hallway, which can be stressful for the fish.

Furthermore, for enhanced visual comfort, the lower portion of the aquarium should ideally be positioned at a height of around 1.30 meters (approximately 4,3 feet), allowing your gaze to rest on the lower half of the tank when you are seated.

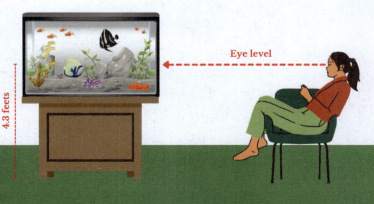

BRINGING AN AQUARIUM TO LIFE

The budget

Given that the passion of aquaristics involves the lives of living beings, it is crucial to have a broad and comprehensive understanding of this hobby. The budget aspect, as with most hobbies, plays a pivotal role in one's appreciation and pursuit of it. Therefore, the ability to quantify and anticipate the expenses associated with this passion is essential to ensure a commitment to embarking on this adventure.

However, establishing a generic price is challenging due to the numerous variables involved. Nonetheless, a fundamental rule that always applies is that the larger the aquarium, the more costly it will be. A larger volume implies a greater demand for raw materials, including larger glass panes for the tank, more substrate, additional decorative elements, and equipment tailored to the tank's size, such as a larger filter and a more powerful lighting system, among others.

The budget will also be significantly influenced by your choices of purchases, whether you opt for new or second-hand items. Additionally, the cost will vary based on your selection of fish species, with popular and budget-friendly species like guppies, platys and bettas on one end, and rarer more expensive species (like Discus, Angelfish, Oscar...).

To provide you with a rough estimate, a minimum budget of **300 to 400$ / 250 to 350£** is advisable for an 20 us gal (80 liters) aquarium when starting from scratch, including equipment and standard fish species.

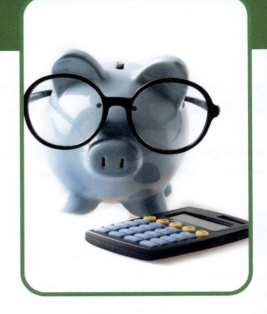

Reduce the bill

Fortunately, there are several strategies to reduce the cost of your aquaristic endeavors. Firstly, turning to the second-hand market can be highly beneficial, both for your wallet and the environment. High-quality equipment is often available at a price significantly lower, typically at least 50% less than the retail price. General or specialized classified ad websites, often provide a wide array of options. The same applies to aquatic plants or even fish, which can be quite costly. You can consider turning to individuals who may part with these items for minimal prices, if not for free. While plants from individuals may be less meticulously presented, often in the form of cuttings without a cultivation pot, they will thrive just as well as those purchased from commercial sources. Moreover, the fish you acquire from individuals may even be in better health.

However, for crucial equipment like filters or LED lighting systems, it is advisable to purchase them new to benefit from the legal warranty in case of malfunction.

Lastly, substantial savings can be achieved by avoiding unnecessary products that are often recommended, such as water conditioners, water purifiers, startup bacteria, algicides, and the like. In addition to their questionable effectiveness for some, these products can be adequately substituted by following the guidance provided throughout this guide.

BRINGING AN AQUARIUM TO LIFE

Technique and equipment

Various techniques, ranging from relatively simple to more complex, can be employed to preserve the biological balance of an aquarium optimally. These techniques involve the use of different materials, equipment, and setups, which collectively serve specific functions. In this section, we will explore the most fundamental setup, including essential equipment such as the tank, the pump/filtration system, lighting, and heating. We will also discuss the essential functions that need to be addressed before considering any alternative installations.

Tank selection

As previously discussed, the tank serves as the central component of your setup, around which all other elements will revolve, including technical equipment, types and numbers of fish and plants, the amount of decor and the level of maintenance and care required. In addition to the size, several choices are available when it comes to selecting the tank of your aquarium.

The preferred shape should be rectangular (or possibly cubic in the case of nano aquariums, as discussed on page 91) to provide an ample swimming length, which is essential for the vast majority of fish. You should also ensure an adequate floor area by choosing a tank with lengths and widths that exceed the height.

In general, other shapes such as column-shaped tanks or, worse still, traditional spherical bowls, should be absolutely avoided.

Indeed, the latter options are entirely unsuitable for aquatic life, as they hinder the installation of necessary equipment, make it challenging to maintain biological stability inside and offer very little space for the fish.

When you are a beginner, it is advisable to avoid "partition aquariums" (used, for instance, to divide two spaces in a home) which can be complex to set up, as well as built-in aquariums which are more challenging to maintain. Additionally, you should steer clear of other exotic styles of aquariums, such as those used as coffee tables, as they are ill-suited for the well-being of the fish, just like spherical bowls.

The most common materials for aquariums fall into two categories : glass and PVC-type plastic. Glass is by far the most widely used. Both glass and the silicone used to bond the aquarium's glass panels together are entirely safe for living creatures as they do not interact with the water, releasing no toxic substances into it. Glass is easier to clean, less prone to scratching, and does not change color over time, making it preferable to PVC.

However, a new type of plastic, methacrylate, is becoming increasingly popular for small tanks. It is more malleable, more transparent and easier to repair (scratches can be polished out), making it a good viable alternative to glass.

Technique and equipment

There are numerous possibilities for choosing the tank, as long as they meet these essential criteria. You can opt to purchase a ready-made new tank, a bare one, or one with equipment (we will discuss the necessary specifications for equipment later on), build your own, or acquire a second-hand tank.

Regardless of the choice you make, there are a few critical considerations :

→ Ensure there are no scratches, impacts, or even slight cracks on the glass.

→ Verify the perfect seal of the seams to prevent any leaks, and confirm that the glass thickness is sufficient, at least 8mm.

When it comes to transporting the tank from the place of purchase to your home, you will need to take precautions based on its size. Smaller tanks may not pose any issues, but for larger ones, it's essential to prepare the appropriate equipment. This includes using a utility vehicle for safe loading, using polystyrene, cardboard, or thick blankets to protect it from any impact, and most importantly, having enough hands to carry and position it easily !

In summary, the ideal tank for beginners should ideally be rectangular, with a floor area that surpasses its height and perfectly suited to the dimensions of its support. It is preferably made of glass (although acrylic is an option), and its dimensions and **volume** should meet the needs of the future inhabitants.

For added maintenance convenience and a wider selection of fish, a minimum volume of 20 us gal is advisable when starting out. A lid, compatible and included directly with the aquarium, is a plus. Some fish are known to be jumpers and require a closed tank to prevent any accidents.

Technique and equipment

The basic equipment

The basic equipment comprises all the electrical components necessary for the operation and maintenance of the biological balance in the aquarium, ensuring various vital functions :

 A **submersible heater** to maintain the appropriate temperature.

 Lighting to simulate the day/night cycles, which is crucial for animal behavior and especially for the healthy growth of plants.

 A **pump** equipped with filter media to prevent water stagnation and degradation.

A heater is essential for <u>most tropical fish</u>, which thrive at water temperatures typically ranging from 70 to 83°F. Unless you live in a region with a warm climate year-round or heat your home significantly (which I do not recommend), you will need a heater in your aquarium to maintain the proper water temperature. However, it is crucial to keep the water temperature as stable as possible, avoiding abrupt fluctuations, which can be harmful to the fish's health (risk of thermal shock).

To achieve this, you should opt for a submersible heater with a thermostat that allows you to set it to a chosen temperature value, known as the setpoint temperature. It will activate every time the water temperature falls below this threshold and deactivate when it reaches the desired level.

For the heater's power, you should typically consider 1 Watt (W) for 1 liter of water or 4W for 1 us gall. For instance, plan for a 100W heater for a 100-liter aquarium (calculate 2W per liter if the room where the aquarium is located is below 14°C). Having a heater with higher wattage is not a problem as long as it is equipped with a thermostat. However, be cautious about the dimensions to ensure it fits inside your aquarium, as higher wattage heaters tend to be more sizable.

You should also equip the aquarium with a thermometer to monitor the water temperature regularly. This is useful in case of equipment malfunctions in the heating system or during hot summer weather. As for the placement of the heater within the aquarium, it is ideal to position it as close as possible to the outflow of the filtration pump. The pump will help circulate the heated water and achieve even heat distribution throughout the tank, preventing the creation of temperature imbalances in different areas.

Submersible heater with thermostat

Technique and equipment

Lighting serves two major functions. Firstly, it artificially recreates a day/night cycle. Numerous biochemical and metabolic processes depend on these cycles and regulate animal behavior. In addition, fish lack eyelids and cannot close their eyes to sleep. Disruptions or irregularities in these cycles can disturb them and gradually lead to latent stress, opening the door to diseases.

If the aquarium is located in a room with natural daylight, it theoretically suffices for the animals (although it is not recommended). However, natural plants have specific light requirements, which can vary in their level of demand. In this case, artificial lighting is essential for the plants. While all types of lighting provide illumination, they are not all equivalent.

Several criteria characterize the various lighting options :

➡ **Type** : T8 or T5 fluorescent tubes, compact fluorescent bulbs, or LEDs. All three can be used, but LED lighting systems are now predominantly found in the market. LEDs have the advantages of lower electricity consumption, longer lifespan, and less heat emission, all while providing equivalent light intensity.

➡ **Power** (in Watts) or more precisely, luminous power (luminous flux) in Lumens : It is important to distinguish between these two values, as they are commonly displayed on lighting systems.

Power in Watts (W) corresponds to the electrical power consumed by the lighting system to operate. It is primarily used to estimate the costs associated with electricity consumption for lighting, and... that's about it ! It was historically used as a reference with fluorescent tube technology (T8 or T5). However, it was an imprecise estimation even then for sizing one's lighting system, and it is even more so today with LED technology. This is because it implied that the efficiency of lamps was the same for all systems, meaning that all lamps produced the same amount of light for the same electrical consumption. In reality, this is not the case.

Today, we can clearly notice the difference when touching a fluorescent tube on one hand and an LED light fixture on the other. The fluorescent tube generates significantly more heat, while the LED does not heat up nearly as much. A portion of the electrical energy (i.e., the Watts) is actually dissipated as heat, and this loss varies between different types of equipment. As a result, a system with T5 fluorescent tubes, for example, dissipates much less heat than a T8 system (indicating better efficiency). Even among T8 systems, the efficiency can vary depending on the quality of the fixtures used. Therefore, using electrical power as the sole basis for decision-making is erroneous.

LEDs, in contrast, have much higher efficiency today. For equivalent light intensity to a T5 fluorescent tube, an LED consumes three times less electrical power. For example, for 600 lumens of light output, a T5 tube consumes around 15W, whereas LEDs consume only about 5W.

ALERT — Be cautious with certain LED lighting systems that do not provide information on lumens or color temperature (as discussed below). Without these crucial values to determine compatibility with your aquarium's needs, you might end up with overly powerful lighting and/or an unsuitable color rendering (especially with blue LEDs, which are better suited for saltwater aquariums), which could promote algae issues. Also, be wary of excessively inexpensive fixtures, as they often reflect low quality and a very limited lifespan.

Technique and equipment

→ **Color temperature** (in °Kelvin) : This aspect is more straightforward to understand, as it determines the hue or color of the lighting. It can range from warm light, which has a pinkish or orangish tone (between 2000 and 3000° Kelvin), to cool light with a bluish hue (10,000° Kelvin) and everything in between, including neutral white light, similar to sunlight (between 4000 and 7000° Kelvin). This parameter is typically considered when choosing lighting for a room in your home to create a specific ambiance, as selecting a color temperature that is too cool can make the room resemble a hospital corridor. However, for our aquarium application, we should opt for lighting with color temperatures close to that of sunlight, typically between 6000 and 8000° Kelvin.

→ **C**olor **R**endering **I**ndex (CRI) is a characteristic directly related to color temperature. It is measured on a scale from 0 to 100% and determines the quality of color reproduction. The higher the CRI, closer to 100%, the more accurately the lighting replicates the color temperature specified in the lamp's technical data.

How to choose suitable lighting ?

As discussed earlier, it's crucial to consider the criteria mentioned above, with a preference for LED lighting, a color temperature close to that of sunlight, and the highest possible CRI (at least 85%). The choice of power should then be determined by the lighting needs of your tank, which are influenced by the quantity of plants. Commonly accepted values are as follows :

- Lightly planted aquarium = 25 lumens per liter
- Moderately planted aquarium = 30 lumens per liter
- Heavily planted aquarium = 40 lumens per liter

For example, in the case of a 26 us gal tank that you want heavily planted, you would need a total light intensity of around 3500 lumens (40 lumens x 100 liters / 26 us gall = 4000 lumens).
Incorrectly sized lighting (too much or too little light) is often a (but not necessarily the only) cause of numerous issues, especially in terms of algae proliferation. We will address this pervasive problem that affects any aquarium hobbyist in the section on "Common Problems and Solutions" on page 72.

Spot LEDs on bracket

LEDs on ramp

Technique and equipment

Filtration is vital for the aquarium and its biological balance. It acts as the wastewater treatment plant, maintaining a healthy and sustainable environment for the fish while relieving you of some maintenance tasks. It should run continuously and only be shut down for cleaning, along with the aquarium.
An aquarium filter consists of several components :
- A motorized pump, which is the powered element responsible for water intake and outflow.
- One or more filter media through which the water, drawn in by the pump, circulates and is purified.

Filtration serves various functions, including mechanical filtration, which involves capturing and trapping suspended waste and particles in the aquarium. It also includes biological filtration, where compounds toxic to aquatic life (resulting from organic waste) are broken down into less harmful compounds (known as the nitrogen cycle, see page 45). A third type, chemical filtration, may be employed for specific needs only, such as removing medication residues after treatment or altering certain chemical water parameters.

To fulfill these functions effectively, the filtration system must meet specific criteria.

➡ **Appropriate Flow Rate** : This rate depends on the aquarium's size, population density and the level of pollution generated by it. Generally, a flow rate of 3 to 5 times of the aquarium's volume per hour is recommended. For a non-overcrowded 26 us gal aquarium with small fish, a filter with a flow rate of 80 g/hour should be sufficient.

➡ **Suitable filter media** : You may have noticed that filters often consist of different-looking "sponges" and filter media. This isn't for aesthetic purposes but rather for technical reasons. Some sponges are designed for mechanical filtration (such as white filter floss or blocks of coarse blue sponge), while others are intended for biological filtration (usually solid and porous materials like small gravel, beads, balls or rings made from materials such as lava rock, ceramic, clay, or sintered glass).
Filters designed for chemical purification typically include blocks of black activated carbon sponge, active peat, or resins (anti-phosphates, anti-nitrates, etc.).

Your filter should consist of components that allow both <u>mechanical and biological filtration.</u>

Internal filter at aquarium bottom

Technique and equipment

Operating principle and filtration configuration

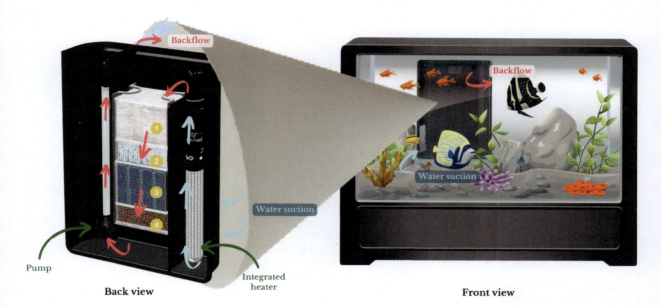

Back view — Pump, Integrated heater

Front view

All types of filters consist of one or more stages of filter media. For the filter above, which is an internal overflow filter with integrated heating, it is composed of :

1 First, there is a pre-filtering foam (filter floss) that captures larger debris (mechanical filtration).

2 The second type of filter media enables bio-mechanical filtration. In this case, ceramic noodles are used. Their shape allows them to trap certain impurities, and their porosity promotes the attachment of bacteria for biological filtration.

3 The third type of filter media captures micro-particles (fine foam). Due to the small mesh size, it also provides a surface for bacteria to attach, contributing to bio-mechanical filtration.

4 The final type of filter media (clay balls) maximizes biological filtration by offering substantial surface area for beneficial bacteria colonization.

It's crucial that the water flow follows this specific path in the order described above.

> If you opt for an aquarium with an internal overflow filter, be cautious about the quality of the plastic used for it. More and more bases are thermoformed from polyethylene plastic due to industrial processes and cost considerations. However, this type of plastic is less effective in adhering to silicone. Consequently, it may eventually come off from the glass, potentially causing problems, especially if the aquarium is in operation.
> To avoid this issue, choose an overflow made from ABS plastic. In addition to being recyclable, it adheres perfectly to silicone and doesn't detach. You can differentiate between the two plastics by lightly wiping them with a tissue soaked in acetone or nail polish remover. ABS plastic tends to dissolve slightly, leaving a black trace on the tissue, while polyethylene remains intact.

Technique and equipment

For other types of filtration (excluding decantation):

Internal

+
- Noise level (varies by model)
- Discretion (varies by model)
- Ease of use
- Effective filtration capacity suitable for small to medium-sized tanks (less than 200 liters)

−
- Occupy a significant portion of the usable volume in the aquarium
- Maintenance more cumbersome
- May have inadequate filtration capacity for larger aquariums

External

+
- Efficiency (essential for larger volumes)
- Maintenance
- Does not occupy any significant space within the aquarium

−
- Risk of leaks
- Installation (priming)
- Requires storage space
- Price

Waterfall

+
- Does not occupy essential space
- Ease of maintenance
- Adjustable suction pipe at water level

−
- Noisy (it lives up to its name as waterfall)
- Not very discreet
- Limited filtration capacity
- Prevents the use of a cover on the aquarium

Exhausteur

+
- Suitable for small volumes
- Price
- Safer for small fish and shrimp (no risk of suction)
- No electrical hazard when in contact with water

−
- To be paired with an air stone, which can vary in noise level depending on the model
- Low flow and limited filtration capacity
- Depletes water of CO_2 and can impact pH

In order to make the best choice for the filter type, it is essential to consider the one that aligns most with the aquarium's requirements (filtration capacity, volume, shape, etc.) and any potential constraints (space, noise, accessibility, etc).

Technique and equipment

Additional elements

In addition to the basic electrical equipment, you will need several additional elements, both mandatory and optional, to perfectly set up an aquarium. For each of these, there are various alternatives to choose from according to your preferences and needs, which we will discuss shortly.
Some of these elements include :

 Substrate, which forms the bottom of the aquarium and serves as a bacterial refuge

 Plants, playing a crucial role in maintaining the ecosystem's health.

 "Hardscape" forming the foundation of aquarium decoration with stones, pebbles, and wood roots.

 Water, an essential and fundamental element that requires an in-depth understanding of its physicochemical characteristics.

All the elements mentioned above make up the complete configuration of an aquarium, allowing you to balance both practical and aesthetic functions. Let's explore these elements in detail, explaining their roles and how to use them effectively.

A natural decor

◀ The combination of various decorative elements, such as a lava stone adorned with Cameroon moss and three *Bucephalandra brownie jade* plants, enables the creation of unique aquatic environments.

The aquarium substrate can consist of various materials and layers, serving multiple functions. Firstly, and primarily in terms of aesthetic appeal, it plays a crucial role by offering opportunities to play with its color and granule size. This enables the creation of contrasts to enhance the colors of both the vegetation and fish, contributing to the desired natural appearance. Additionally, the substrate allows plants to establish their roots properly and, in some cases, provides essential nutrients for their growth. Furthermore, it plays a significant role in the biological balance of the tank, as it hosts a substantial colony of bacteria that purify the water, much like the filter.

While there are no specific precautions to consider regarding the various substrates that can be used, it is essential to understand the characteristics of each type to select the one or ones that best suit your tank :

➡ **Porous Substrates** : Typically made from crushed volcanic rock (like pumice) or clay pellets, these substrates are beneficial for use as the first layer of the substrate. They allow for easy volume adjustment, promote soil drainage, and, due to their porosity, facilitate plant root growth and serve as a significant bacterial refuge for biological water purification. A generous layer of this type of substrate can and should be used.

➡ **Neutral Substrates** : These substrates can be of different types (e.g. sand, quartz, basalt, ...) and are termed 'neutral' because they do not alter any parameters in the tank (neither water parameter changes nor nutrient release for plants). Their value lies primarily in aesthetics, with various color intensities available, ranging from very light white to very dark black, as well as different granule sizes. These should be applied at a depth of 5-6 cm (2 - 2,4 inch).

Technique and equipment

→ Soil (technical soil) : This substrate consists of reconstituted terracotta pellets, containing a variety of nutrients for plants. It's referred to as "technical" because when used with osmosis water (RO), it can directly impact water parameters, making the water slightly acidic with very low hardness. These modifications are necessary in specific cases, such as breeding certain shrimp species or for creating 'Aquascaping' style layouts. Otherwise, it has limited relevance and is too complex for regular beginner use.

→ Soil fertilizer : Often likened to garden soils, they serve the same purpose but are specially designed for aquariums (never use garden soil in an aquarium !). Composed of a blend of mineral-rich sands and nutrients, their sole purpose is to provide plants with everything they need to grow. They should be placed as a sub-layer beneath a neutral-type substrate, with a sufficiently substantial thickness (between 5 and 8 cm / 2 to 3 inch) to prevent the soil fertilizer from surfacing. A soil fertilizer is almost mandatory for some demanding plants.

For most substrates (except soil fertilizer and soil), it is recommended to rinse them thoroughly with clear water before placing them in the aquarium to remove any impurities and dust they may contain

ⓘ Unless you have a specific reason to do so (hospital tank, quarantine tank, or breeding tank), it is strongly discouraged not to use any substrate in the aquarium. If you are a beginner and unsure of your choice, it is advisable to opt for sand, which will be suitable for any type of aquarium

Technique and equipment

The choice of substrate should be based on your expectations in terms of aesthetic appeal, as well as the level of planting and the type of fish you intend to keep in your aquarium. Some species may not be compatible with certain substrates. For example, fish such as Cichlids or goldfish, known for their "bulldozing behavior", are not suitable for a planted substrate with a soil fertilizer, as it will quickly be disturbed. In such cases, you should choose a 100% neutral substrate that allows fish to dig and disturb the substrate without any risks. Similarly, bottom-dwelling fish like Corydoras may not be compatible with a neutral substrate like quartz, which can be abrasive and pose a risk of injuring their barbels.

Setting up the substrate is not complicated but can be done in different ways. Firstly, you can opt for the simplest method of a single-layer substrate, which can be either 100% neutral substrate for a straightforward setup or 100% "technical" soil for specific requirements (precise water parameters for the intended fish species or nutrients for a densely planted tank).

However, if your aquarium setup or future plant population demands it, you may need to use a multi-layer substrate. This process should **always** follow the sequence below :

<u>1st layer</u> : Porous substrate, such as crushed lava rock, if used. This substrate can be spread directly at the bottom of the aquarium or placed in advance in nets, like potato mesh bags, to prevent any rising to the surface (which can occur if using a top substrate with a fine granule size, like sand and insufficient depth). It's recommended to use a substantial layer, especially if you want to give volume to your substrate.

<u>2nd layer</u> : Soil fertilizer, if the top visible layer will be a neutral substrate and you desire demanding plants. Cover the porous substrate directly with the soil fertilizer to a depth of about 2-3 cm (1 to 1,5 inch). It's possible for the finer soil fertilizer to spread into the gaps of the porous substrate or slide beneath it. This isn't problematic, as the plant roots will reach it to extract nutrients, and some of them will also be released directly into the water."

▲ View of one of the normally concealed sides of an aquarium with a two-layer substrate : a layer of pumice (in red) covered by a layer of light quartz (in green). Some gravel is protruding here due to insufficient depth of the quartz layer.

Technique and equipment

For the lower substrates, which serve a functional rather than aesthetic purpose, it is recommended not to attach them to the glass to prevent the distinct separation of the different layers later on (as shown in previous illustrations). To achieve this, leave a gap of approximately 1 cm between the glass walls and the island formed by the first layers of substrate (illustration in the section - Setting up your first aquarium - page 53).

<u>3rd layer</u> : The final and visible layer is placed on top of the others using a neutral substrate. To prevent any rising of the lower layers, it's advisable to distribute a sufficiently thick layer, with a thickness of at least 4/5 cm (1,5 to 2 inch).

> ⓘ To reduce the budget allocated to substrate (which can increase significantly for larger aquariums), it's possible to consider substrates not marketed specifically for aquarium use, which tend to be more expensive. For instance, you can purchase crushed lava rock intended for gardening as mulch or ground cover, or use pool filter sand instead of aquarium sand. Just make sure to verify that the intended substrate is natural, free from any chemical treatment and safe for your fish.

The substrates presented here are just examples among the most commonly found and easily available in the market. In reality, there is a wide and diverse range of substrates, each belonging to one of the mentioned substrate types. There are also substrates that can combine multiple functions (aesthetic and nutritive, as seen with technical soil, or porous and nutritive as in the case of Aqualit for example). It's up to you to clearly define your expectations and needs regarding your aquarium's substrate and then choose the most suitable one from the variety available.

Substrates to avoid

Artificially colored quartz
The paint used to artificially color this quartz can potentially be harmful to the aquarium in the long run, as it may release certain harmful substances into the water.

Coral sand
Intended for marine aquariums, coral sand, composed of crushed calcium-rich shells, will significantly impact water parameters in a freshwater aquarium, leading to excessive hardness and pH levels.

Seashore sand
Like coral sand, the sand found along our coasts contains a significant amount of calcium-rich shells (in addition to potential parasites). Moreover, it is often illegal to collect from nature.

"Technical" soil
For beginners, it is not recommended to use this complex type of substrate due to the negatives mentioned in the previous chart.

Technique and equipment

Hardscape encompasses all the elements that form the foundation of your aquarium's decor : wood roots, stones, pebbles, and more. Their primary purpose is to enhance the aesthetics of your tank, but they can also potentially serve as hiding places for some of the inhabitants. While the arrangement is entirely up to your preferences, there are a few rules to consider when selecting the various objects that make up the decor.

➡ Wooden roots can be purchased or collected from nature. Most types of wood can be used, except for conifers (such as spruce, fir, and pine). In both cases, but especially when collecting from nature, it's essential to ensure that no harmful elements (fungi, bacteria, parasites, etc) accompany the roots into your tank. A soak in boiling water for one to two hours will eliminate any potential risks.

Furthermore, this process will saturate the roots with water, making them sink more easily (if that's not sufficient, you can weigh them down with a stone, for example, until they no longer float) and remove a significant portion of the tannins responsible for the amber discoloration of the water. If your root is too large to fully submerge in your hot water container, you can soak it side by side : first, immerse one part for an hour before flipping the root so that the previously unimmersed section is submerged for an hour as well.

The most popular roots

Mangrove root
The most well-known and commonly used variety in aquariums. It contains a high amount of tannins that have the effect of acidifying and coloring the water, which is appreciated by Amazonian fish.

Spider wood
A root that has become increasingly popular thanks to aquascaping. This type of root is ideal for creating aerial or woody scapes adorned with epiphytic plants like Anubias, Bucephalandra, or Java moss. Its light-colored wood and lower tannin content have minimal impact on the water.

Mopani root
Recognizable by its distinctive two-tone coloring, this root can come in various sizes and shapes. It is particularly favored by plants that can easily root themselves on it.

'Bonsai tree' root
Bonsai trees are becoming more common, with roots carefully assembled by hand to mimic real bonsai trees. The addition of moss on the tips of the finer branches recreates the foliage of trees once it has grown.

ⓘ It's worth noting that it's normal to observe the growth of white mold (actually mycelium) on the roots during the first few weeks of immersion in the aquarium water. Depending on the animal population present, these should be consumed fairly quickly. You can also remove them during routine water changes.

Technique and equipment

→ Stones, rocks, or pebbles, much like roots, can be bought or collected from your garden when possible. However, you need to be well-informed about their type. In most cases, you should avoid limestone stones, often light and gray, if your aquarium houses fish that require soft and acidic water. Similar to coral or beach sand, limestone stones directly affect water parameters by increasing its pH and hardness to varying degrees.

To determine whether a stone is non-limestone, a simple test involves pouring a few drops of white vinegar or, even better, hydrochloric acid on it. If you observe a reaction that produces small bubbles (with vinegar) or a denser effervescent foam (with hydrochloric acid) then your stone is likely limestone. Stones collected by yourself should be scrubbed, scraped, and ideally boiled to remove potential unwanted inhabitants. Commercial stones may also require a little cleaning to prevent them from introducing any soil or dust into the future aquarium water.

ℹ️ Naturally calcareous elements (such as coral sand, rocks like moonstone, etc.) can be intentionally used to modify water parameters, notably increasing hardness and pH. However, this is only relevant in specific cases, such as private African cichlid aquariums, for instance

The most popular stones

Volcanic stones
Lava Stone or Galapagos, both types of volcanic rocks have a very natural appearance and the advantage of high porosity, promoting the colonization of water-purifying bacteria and being entirely neutral. They are easily breakable to suit desired shapes.

Seiryu Stone
One of the most commonly used types of rock in aquaristics (especially in aquascaping). With a gray to slightly bluish color, it's particularly suitable for recreating mountainous landscapes. Note that it is slightly calcareous.

Dragon Stone
Similar to Seiryu Stone, Dragon Stone is a natural rock with ochre/orange hues. Also known as Okho Stone, it's commonly used in aquascaping to recreate various landscapes. It's easily breakable and neutral in terms of water parameters.

Slate
Aesthetic flat and thin tile-shaped stone, generally dark in color, allowing for a unique appearance when stacked on top of each other. Easily breakable and neutral in terms of water parameters.

Leopard Stone
Smooth stone with gray and white hues and stripes. It has a very natural appearance in an aquarium without altering water parameters. However, it's rather sturdy, making it difficult to modify from its original form.

Plants

Live plants are an essential component of the aquarium. Besides the aesthetic, natural, and decorative aspect they bring, a significant vegetation exerts an **exclusively positive influence** on the aquarium's ecosystem. Just like on Earth, plants contribute to sustaining animal life (including humans) through a unique biochemical process: photosynthesis. Using light energy, carbon dioxide (CO_2), and certain nutrients like nitrates, plants can generate all the energy they need to live and grow while releasing oxygen as their sole waste product, which we breathe.

In an aquarium, this process is exactly the same. Introduced plants thrive with the provided lighting and the CO_2 naturally present in the water (although it can be artificially increased to enhance plant growth) while releasing the necessary oxygen for fish respiration into the aquarium water. That's why in aquariums with lush vegetation, air stones are entirely unnecessary.

Of course, this process doesn't occur at night in the absence of light. Plants switch to a respiration process similar to ours, absorbing oxygen (O_2) and exhaling carbon dioxide (CO_2). In some cases, this can pose a few issues, especially if a CO_2 injection system, as mentioned earlier, is used and continues to release carbon dioxide when not correctly regulated, even at night.

This overproduction of CO_2 can have potentially deadly consequences for the animals, leading to two combined phenomena: asphyxiation (due to a decrease in oxygen levels displaced by the injected CO_2) and acidosis (resulting in a decrease in pH).

In normal operation (with a well-regulated CO_2 system if used), suitable water parameters, and healthy plants, the amount of oxygen released during the day by the plants is greater than that absorbed by them at night. This prevents any risk of oxygen depletion and asphyxiation for the fish.

In addition to their vital biochemical action, live plants provide ideal hiding and feeding places for fish, especially juveniles. Mosses, such as the famous Java Moss (*Taxiphyllum barbieri*), are particularly interesting in this regard, as they support the development of numerous microorganisms within them, serving as basic food for fry.

An aquarium that's not short of air ... or plants !

The needs of plants, just like those of animals, must be met for them to develop properly. Firstly, it's essential to ensure that the lighting is properly tailored to the tank (refer to the 'Lighting' section on page 18), as it's the most important factor. Initially, provide relatively low lighting for the first few weeks (about 7 hours per day), gradually increasing to 10 to 12 hours of lighting per day (adding 30 minutes to 1 hour of additional lighting per week starting from the third week is a good compromise).

Next, there are other criteria that are less important but still vital (a deficiency in any of them can slow down plant growth or lead to their decline). These include maintaining an appropriate temperature, water with suitable parameters (pH, KH, GH, CO_2), and providing the right amount of nutrients – not too much or too little (nitrates, phosphates, potassium, iron, copper, etc.).

Two types of deficiencies are commonly recognized as reasons for stunted growth or the death of a plant :

– A deficiency due to the absence of a necessary nutrient, which is relatively simple to address with appropriate lighting and fertilization.

– An induced deficiency, resulting from the plant's inability to assimilate a specific type of nutrient. This typically occurs when there is an imbalanced pH (outside the range of 6 – 8) or an imbalance related to the quantity of certain elements (e.g., excessive nitrates, too much light, insufficient iron, potassium, etc., preventing the assimilation of another nutrient due to a lack of synergy).

Nutrients are primarily supplied by water. However, supplementary nutrients can be beneficial or even essential for certain demanding plants through the use of a technical soil (or a soil fertilizer beneath a neutral substrate, as explained in the 'Substrate' section on page 23) or by adding liquid fertilizers directly to the water.

▲ Close observation of the plants can help detect deficiencies. For example, in this image, severe iron chlorosis is visible on the hygrophila, indicated by the yellowing of older leaves due to a deficiency of iron.

▲ A plant that "bubbles" is a sign of good health; it indicates that the plant has all the necessary nutrients, including CO_2. This phenomenon is typically observed after the addition of a CO_2 injection system.

Plants

A non-exhaustive chart listing some potential issues that may arise with your plants due to potential nutrient deficiencies.

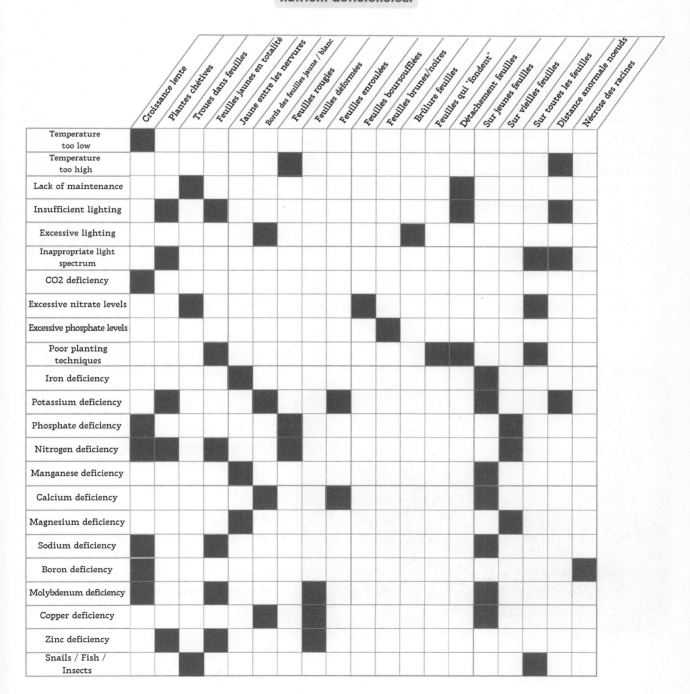

The selection of plants is the next crucial step in creating a harmonious aquarium environment. To achieve this, it's essential to diversify the plant species within the tank. Opt for larger plants in the background, medium-sized ones for the middle area, and smaller plants for the foreground. Additionally, your choice should be guided by the aquarium's characteristics, taking into account its size to ensure that the selected plants have enough room to grow. It's equally important to consider the lighting intensity. If your aquarium lacks strong illumination, you should lean towards relatively undemanding plants.

Furthermore, when selecting plants, it's wise to strike a balance between fast-growing species, which can compete with and limit algae development during the initial phase, and slow-growing plants to avoid depleting essential nutrients, which can lead to deficiencies.

For your convenience, we've compiled comprehensive information about the main plant species, including their types, planting instructions, and care requirements, in the "Plant sheets" section on page 119. Carefully review these sheets as if they were a catalog, helping you choose plants that best suit your preferences and needs.

Purchasing your plants is a critical step which not to be underestimated. The quality of the plants you acquire will directly impact their ability to adapt and thrive once they are planted in your aquarium. Therefore, it is imperative to be meticulous in your selection choosing only healthy specimens without yellowing or damaged leaves, free from holes and even minimal traces of algae. Don't hesitate to invest several minutes in scrutinizing each plant if necessary. Your time investment at this stage will save you a host of future issues and ensure a flourishing aquatic environment.

The "dry start" method is a specialized technique for launching an aquarium that, as the name suggests, does not involve the use of water initially. While it may seem unusual at first, this method offers numerous advantages, particularly when it comes to **the acclimatization and growth** of certain plants.

First and foremost, it's crucial to understand that the majority of plants sold in the field of aquaristics are, in reality, not true aquatic plants but rather marsh plants. These plants thrive in a humid environment and are artificially submerged. Before they reach our stores, they are typically grown in their original, emersed form, often in production farms primarily located in Southeast Asia. This practice is driven by cost and efficiency considerations - these farms benefit from natural light, which is not available in artificial aquarium setups, more atmospheric CO_2, and the absence of algae growth in open air.

The dry start method essentially replicates this concept. An aquarium is set up conventionally (as explained in the "Setting up your first aquarium" section on page 51) but without water, or with only a minimal amount. The aquarium is partially filled with water, primarily through misting during plant placement to prevent desiccation, and then topped up to achieve a water level equal to that of the substrate. In this method, the plants (stems and leaves) must remain exposed to the air, with the substrate barely covered with water. Once everything is in place, the aquarium is covered, either with its lid or, even better, with plastic wrap to maintain high humidity. The lighting is programmed for 8 to 10 hours per day, and you must wait for 4 to 8 weeks, regularly moistening the interior of the aquarium to ensure it remains never completely dry. This approach allows the plants to establish themselves more quickly within the aquarium, making them more competitive against algae when you eventually introduce water.

BRINGING AN AQUARIUM TO LIFE

Water

Water is, without a doubt, the primary and most crucial element in an aquarium. Its chemical composition and quality must be perfectly suited to maintain a sustainable ecosystem, ensure the health of the fish, and preserve the long-term aesthetic appeal of the aquarium. As we've discussed, ensuring water quality involves effective mechanical and biological filtration. However, there are a number of chemical parameters, some of which are influenced by filtration, while others are independent, that need regular monitoring. To guarantee that your water quality remains optimal, it is imperative to conduct water tests, particularly for all the parameters outlined in this section.

H2O molecules, but not only ...

In chemistry, pure water is a substance composed solely of H_2O molecules, consisting of two hydrogen atoms and one oxygen. However, outside of a chemistry laboratory, it is exceedingly rare to encounter naturally occurring pure water.

Water is a solvent that collects various elements during its natural cycle, known as the water cycle. Under the influence of the Earth's internal heat and sunlight, liquid water on Earth evaporates to form clouds. When these high-altitude clouds encounter cooler air masses, they condense into liquid droplets and fall as rain or snow, eventually returning to the Earth's surface, either above or below ground (in streams, lakes, rivers, seas, and aquifers). The different pathways water takes and its interactions with the Earth's layers, or with our domestic water supply systems, which can include rocks, organic materials, or metals, significantly influence its composition. Therefore, depending on the course of liquid water and its final destination before evaporation or condensation, its chemical composition can vary greatly. In this section, what we refer to as "water parameters" will encompass certain key characteristics that reflect the physico-chemical properties of water and are directly dependent on its composition.

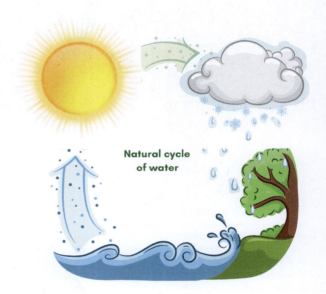

Natural cycle of water

> ℹ️ The phenomenon of acid rain is also a consequence of the water cycle. In certain industrial or volcanic regions, the release of specific substances into the atmosphere, such as nitrogen oxides and sulfur oxides, leads to the acidification of water vapor within the clouds as these substances dissolve in it. Subsequently, when this acidified water vapor falls as precipitation, it is termed as acid rain, with a pH level below 5.

Water testing in aquarium keeping

To ensure the quality of your water and to identify any deviations, it is essential to regularly test your aquarium water, at a minimum of once a month and even bimonthly for certain parameters like pH. These tests can be conducted using various methods, including test strips, liquid reagent kits, electronic devices, and more. The method of choice for the best accuracy at a reasonable cost is often the liquid reagent tests. In the market, you can find a variety of tests designed to monitor different parameters. Of course, not all parameters are of equal importance. For cost-effectiveness, you can focus on obtaining the following essential tests :

- GH (General Hardness)
- pH (Hydrogen Potential)
- KH (Carbonate Hardness)
- Nitrites (NO2)

And, if possible, consider :

- Nitrates (NO3)
- Phosphates (PO4)
- Ammonia (NH4)

You can purchase these tests as a set in a kit, which can significantly reduce the total acquisition cost.

Useful information

You have the option to perform water tests on your own by purchasing your own kits, but these can often be expensive. Another solution is to take a sample of your aquarium water to a pet store, and many of them are willing to conduct the test(s) for you, typically free of charge. However, it's worth noting that these tests are often carried out using test strips, which contain reagents and require placing a drop of aquarium water on them. The drawback of this type of test is that they can be imprecise and even entirely inaccurate. It's advisable to request tests using liquid reagents or seek out a pet store that employs this method if your regular pet store does not offer it.

Water

General hardness (GH)

GH (General hardness) measures the mineral content of water, primarily the salts of calcium and magnesium. Depending on the concentrations of these different minerals present, water can range from very soft to very hard. This phenomenon is what explains why, in various regions, the course and source of water, varying amounts of soap are needed to produce lather when washing hands, for example. Soft water requires only a small amount of soap, while hard water necessitates a larger quantity.

In our aquariums, total hardness plays a direct role in biological processes, specifically osmosis. Osmosis is a biochemical phenomenon that explains the flow of pure water through a permeable membrane, separating two aqueous solutions with different concentrations. In other words, it is the ability to balance two waters with varying mineral concentrations on either side of a membrane between two aqueous solutions at the same concentrations.

This phenomenon occurs due to the different pressures at play between the two liquids. The liquid with a higher concentration exerts a greater pressure, known as osmotic pressure, on the membrane separating the two liquids. This pressure facilitates the movement of water from the less concentrated liquid to the more concentrated one, with the aim of equalizing the concentration on both sides of the membrane. This process continues until the concentrations of both liquids are balanced on either side.

Osmotic pressure affects all living organisms, whether animals or plants. In humans, it operates within the body at the cellular level, facilitating the transport of nutrients and maintaining intra- and extracellular pressures within biological systems.

For aquatic organisms, osmotic pressure plays a direct role in their interaction with the environment, i.e., water. Fish possess an osmoregulation system finely tuned to the water hardness in their natural habitat. This system enables them to compensate and adjust the mineral concentration in their bodies based on the mineral concentration in the water where they reside. If the GH is too low, the water lacks sufficient minerals to assist the fish in osmoregulation, potentially leading to metabolic disorders, bone deformities, or reproductive issues. Conversely, if the water is too hard, it can cause problems with fish respiration, lead to salt accumulations in the kidneys and gills, or increase the risk of diseases. These issues can even arise in slightly unsuitable water. In water that is entirely unsuitable for the species' living conditions, the consequences can be more severe, possibly leading to the fish's death due to **osmotic shock**.

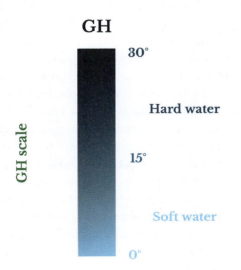

This is why it is essential to ensure that the water parameters are suitable for the species living in your aquarium and to avoid significant and/or sudden fluctuations.

Hydrogen potential or pH

Another critical characteristic of water, pH, is also one of the most vital parameters in aquarium keeping due to the high sensitivity of aquatic life to it. While most people have heard of pH at least once, it's rarer to precisely understand what it represents.

In chemistry, pH, or potential hydrogen, is a measurement that determines the acidity level of a liquid, determined by the quantity of hydroxide ions it contains. It is measured on a scale ranging **from 0 to 14**. The closer the value is to 0, the more acidic the environment is. As an example, sodas typically have a pH of around 3. Conversely, as the pH value approaches 14, the environment is considered alkaline (or basic). Between these two extreme values, around 7, the pH is labeled as neutral.

Most fish thrive in water with a neutral pH or water that is slightly acidic or slightly alkaline, typically between 6 and 8. However, some species require very acidic pH levels (as low as 4.5 for certain Amazonian fish) while others prefer higher pH levels (up to 8.5 for fish from some African great lakes). This underscores the importance of researching the specific water requirements of the species you intend to keep and adjusting the pH (as well as other parameters) accordingly.

accordingly. Beyond the absolute pH value (as long as it falls within a reasonable range), it's the abrupt fluctuations that can be most dangerous for the animals. This holds particularly true for pH but also applies to other parameters such as temperature.

To understand the sensitivity of pH, it's crucial to grasp the unique nature of the pH scale. The scale used is not linear but logarithmic (apologies for breaking the "no more math" promise in the first chapter - I promise this is the last time!). The difference between the two scales lies in the value of one unit. Consider this example: to move from 1 to 2 on a linear scale, we add a unit equal to 1 (1 + 1 = 2), making a value of "2" twice as large as "1" (2 x 1 = 2). Now, on a logarithmic scale, this unit is no longer equal to 1 but 10. This results in a value ten times greater between 1 and 2. In our case, a pH of 7 is ten times higher than a pH of 6, meaning the water is ten times less acidic. Conversely, a pH of 6 is ten times lower, meaning the water is ten times more acidic. Similarly, a pH of 8 is 100 times higher than a pH of 6.

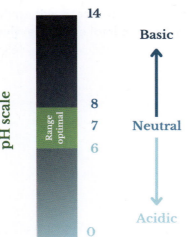

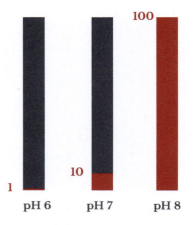

A pH of 8 will be 10x higher than a pH of 7 and 100x higher than a pH of 6.

Water

Measuring pH will be an essential task in your life as an aquarium enthusiast. It must be performed before introducing any living organisms into the aquarium and regularly thereafter to anticipate or detect any potential issues. A good frequency for this measurement is once a month.
The use of a drop test is typically preferred, as it offers greater precision than test strips. For even more accuracy, you can opt for electronic pH meters. However, if you are not familiar with this kind of advanced equipment, including calibration, probe cleaning, and maintenance, we advise against using them for the minimal additional benefit they provide in most cases.

The drop test involves adding a reactive solution to a flask containing a precise amount of aquarium water, usually 5 ml. Another flask filled with aquarium water serves as a control flask. After adding the reagent to one of the two flasks, the water will change color within a few minutes. Once the color stabilizes, you can compare it to a color scale provided, which features various chromatographic patches, each corresponding to a pH value. Once you identify the match, you can read the associated pH value.

It is possible that if you conduct multiple pH tests throughout the same day, you may obtain different values. This is normal as long as the variation remains slight (a few tenths of a difference at most) with the pH typically being at its highest in the morning before the lights come on and at its lowest in the evening after the lights go out.

The explanation of these normal pH fluctuations throughout the day introduces two other key water parameters directly related to the parameters discussed earlier : **carbonate hardness** (KH) and **carbon dioxide** (CO_2).

> When adding a CO_2 injection system, it is crucial to regularly check pH values with a test just before the lights are switched on and another just before they are turned off.

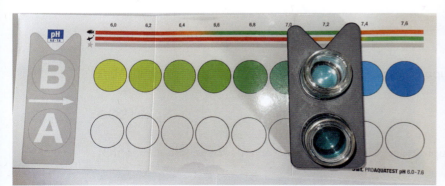

▲ Colour chart, enabling the pH value to be read according to the colour obtained after the reagent has been added.

▲ Difference in colour between two waters with different pH values, following the addition of the reagent.

Carbonate hardness

Carbonate hardness (KH) is a component of the total hardness (GH) that can represent up to 80% of it. In some cases, especially for water with high pH levels, it's possible for the KH to be higher than the GH, influenced by certain minerals like sodium and potassium, which are not accounted for in some test measurements.

Carbonate hardness measures only the level of calcium and magnesium carbonates in the water, specifically hydrogen carbonate ions, also known as bicarbonates. This parameter is crucial in an aquarium because it directly affects pH by preventing or mitigating pH fluctuations. This property is referred to as buffering capacity or the ability to dissolve a quantity of acids or bases. Therefore, the higher the KH, the stronger the buffering capacity of the water, making the pH more resistant to changes and more stable. To modify the pH of water, you must first lower the KH, reducing its resistance to pH fluctuations. A KH greater than 4 or 5 prevents any dangerous pH swings.

Measuring KH should be done simultaneously with pH measurement to provide an accurate and comprehensive understanding of your water's composition.

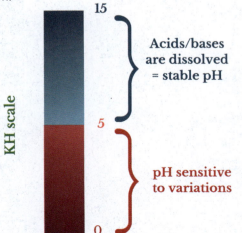

Carbon dioxide (CO2)

Carbon dioxide (CO_2) is essential in aquariums to promote the healthy growth of plants by playing a key role in photosynthesis. However, what we are concerned with here is the relationship it represents between the pH and KH of the aquarium water.

These three parameters are directly interconnected, and this connection can be easily observed, especially in heavily planted aquariums without additional CO_2 supplementation. When the CO_2 requirements of the plants (and algae) in the tank exceed the available CO_2 levels in the water, the plants eventually draw the carbon necessary for their growth from bicarbonate ions (and thus from KH). This phenomenon is known as biogenic decalcification. It can be recognized by the presence of white spots on the plastic parts of the filter or suction cups and, when it becomes critical, on the leaves of the plants. This plant consumption leads to a reduction in the levels of carbonates (and thus a decrease in KH, which measures this quantity) and, in parallel, the production of a certain type of waste: hydroxide ions. This combination of phenomena (decreasing KH and production of hydroxide ions) triggers another chain reaction: a sudden increase in pH.

Biogenic decalcification highlights the constant and interconnected relationship between CO2, KH, and pH. **Therefore, it's essential to interpret these three parameters together, particularly when introducing a CO2 injection system (see the table below).**

Water

Excessive CO2 (ppm) **Correct CO2 level (ppm)** **Not enough CO2 (ppm)**

pH value

KH Value	6,5	6,6	6,7	6,8	6,9	7	7,1	7,2	7,3	7,4	7,5	7,6	7,7
1	10	8	7	5	4	4	3	3	2	2	1	1	1
2	20	16	13	10	8	6	5	4	3	3	2	2	1
3	30	24	19	15	12	10	8	6	5	4	3	3	2
4	40	32	25	20	16	13	10	7	6	5	4	3	3
5	50	40	32	25	20	16	13	10	8	6	5	4	2
6	60	48	38	30	24	19	15	12	10	8	6	5	3
7	70	56	44	35	28	22	18	14	11	9	7	6	4
8	80	64	51	40	32	25	20	16	13	10	8	6	5
9	90	72	57	45	36	29	23	18	14	11	9	7	5
10	100	80	63	50	40	32	25	20	16	13	10	8	6
11	111	88	70	55	44	35	28	22	18	14	11	9	7

Conductivity

The electrical conductivity of water is a concept that is significantly less known and understood compared to other water parameters. However, it can play a vital role and prove to be quite intriguing in the field of aquaristics.

When we refer to the electrical conductivity of water, we are talking about its ability to allow electrical current to pass through more or less easily. This characteristic is directly linked to the presence of minerals. The higher the mineral concentration in the water, the better it conducts electricity. Conversely, water with low mineral content is a poor conductor and will allow electrical current to pass through with difficulty. This applies to all minerals. You can immediately appreciate the additional value that conductivity brings in comparison to GH (General Hardness). While GH measures only the quantity of major minerals such as calcium and magnesium, conductivity takes into account all mineral salts, including calcium and magnesium, as well as sodium, potassium, chlorides, sulfates, nitrates, phosphates, and more. Therefore, it provides a much more precise indication of water mineralization and, by extension, its hardness (the term "total hardness" used for GH is, in reality, inappropriate) and its purity.

To provide a meaningful comparison, let's consider two waters with opposing levels of hardness : rainwater and seawater. The first is very soft with a very low mineral concentration (< 40 ppm). The second, on the other hand, is highly mineralized (> 30 000 ppm), particularly in sodium chloride, which is table salt. By measuring the conductivity of each, we get the following values :

Rainwater : 10 to 40 µS/cm

Ocean water : 50 000 µS/cm or 50 mS/cm

µS stands for microSiemens and mS stands for milliSiemens (Siemens being the unit of measurement for conductance).

The measurement of GH is indeed a less precise indicator of water mineralization compared to electrical conductivity. So, which one should you prioritize? Well, it depends on your aquarium and the sensitivity of the living organisms within it. For most common freshwater fish and plants, adhering to the recommended GH values will suffice. Most of these species are hardy and can adapt to a fairly wide range of parameters. However, for more delicate species like certain shrimp or, in general, marine organisms (corals, fish, etc.), this level of precision will be vital for their well-being.

On the other hand, measuring conductivity in freshwater can help you keep a close eye on water quality. It provides a more precise insight into the overall composition of the water, which can indicate a potential issue if there is a significant increase in the measured value (this could result from a spike in nitrite or nitrate pollution, a malfunctioning reverse osmosis system in the case of using RO water, and so on). The limitation of this measurement is that it only offers a comprehensive value and doesn't detail each key parameter (KH, nitrites, nitrates, phosphates, etc.). For these, you will need to maintain separate drop tests.

Conductimeter

Water

Temperature

Temperature may not be the most complicated parameter to measure or maintain (in most cases), but it is equally crucial to monitor to ensure that your inhabitants are kept at the right temperature. Indeed, it directly impacts the health of the fish, whether it's too high or too low.

In the higher range of tolerance (usually around 86°F for most tropical freshwater fish), temperature can significantly reduce the lifespan of individuals due to an acceleration of their metabolism and, consequently, aging. This phenomenon is particularly evident in invertebrates like shrimp, which, when exposed to high temperatures, undergo more frequent molts (resulting in accelerated growth and aging). High temperatures also promote the growth of bacteria, not the beneficial ones, but potentially pathogenic ones (the quantities of good bacteria tend to decrease at higher temperatures due to lower oxygen levels in warmer water, which dissolves less oxygen than cooler water).

Conversely, temperatures that are too low will slow down the metabolism of fish, potentially stunting their growth and weakening their immune system, making them vulnerable to various opportunistic diseases.

So it is imperative to adhere to the recommended temperatures for each species, avoiding extreme values and sudden fluctuations as much as possible. Particularly during the summer, special vigilance is necessary on very hot days that can quickly elevate the aquarium water temperature.

Mercury thermometer

The presence of a thermometer, whether it's a traditional mercury thermometer as shown above or a digital one as depicted below, is essential in any aquarium.

Sticky thermometer

Cooling the water in your aquarium may be necessary during certain periods, especially in the summer. To achieve this, various mthods with varying levels of effectiveness are available. The choice of method will primarily depend on your tank's volume, the intensity of summer heat in your region, and your budget. Here are some possible methods, ranging from the least expensive but less effective to the most efficient and costly :

- Regular water changes with cooler water (avoiding significant temperature variations between the tank water and the new water to prevent thermal shock to the fish; a maximum difference of 37°F is advisable)

- Floating bottles of frozen water directly in the tank (note that this method is often criticized by many aquarists due to the significant thermal differences it introduces between different zones of the aquarium, potentially causing thermal shocks, although some aquarists have reported success with this method).

- Using one or more fans aimed at the water's surface to cool it through forced convection

- Adding an air pump to promote thermal exchange between the air and the water's surface (through the agitation caused by the bubbles) and to oxygenate the water, which tends to decrease with rising temperatures

- Investing in a chiller unit that can cool and maintain a constant water temperature, to be installed directly on the filter outlet (this method works only with external filters)

It's worth noting that several of the methods mentioned above can be used simultaneously for more effective cooling.

Depending on the circumstances, some methods will be more suitable than others. It's essential to anticipate which one will best fit your situation even before you face the need for cooling.

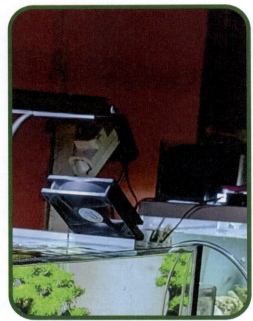

▲ A fan directed towards the surface of the water

▲ The frozen water should be placed **in front of the filter outlet** to prevent the creation of areas with significantly different temperatures, which could potentially lead to thermal shocks.

Modify water parameters

Depending on the parameters of the tap water at your location and the requirements for maintaining fish that match their needs, there may be a small (or significant) gap. In this scenario, you have two options :

The <u>first option</u> is to keep the tap water as it is in your aquarium and select fish species that are compatible.
Pros : installation and maintenance are straightforward.
Cons : the choice of fish may be (very) limited.

The <u>second option</u> is to adapt the future aquarium water to the requirements of the desired fish.
Pros : greater freedom in choosing fish (provided that the tank volume is also suitable).
Cons : implementation and maintenance are more complex, requiring a bit more effort.

The question is worth considering, depending on the level of commitment you want to invest in your aquarium. However, keep in mind that if your tap water is fundamentally unsuitable (for instance, if it contains too many nitrates, NO3 exceeding 20 ppm), you will have no choice but to opt for the second option. But before you dismiss this option, let's take a closer look at what it entails.

In reality, this process involves a simple mixture of tap water, which is typically hard to very hard depending on the region and may have high nitrate levels, and very soft water, such as reverse osmosis water, which is nearly pure water.
This mixture is essentially a dilution of the chemical components in the water to reduce their levels. The first step is to measure the initial parameters of your tap water and compare them to the target parameters you wish to achieve for the aquarium water. Once this is done, you'll need to select the water that will be used in the mixture and determine the proportions of each.

For this purpose, you will need to examine the parameters of the second water. There are several alternatives to consider :

- **Reverse Osmosis (RO) water**, the most commonly used water source for modifying water parameters. As it is almost pure water, it has a GH and KH of zero (no minerals), making it ideal for lowering hardness in any water. You can either purchase it directly from a pet store for a few cents per liter or produce it yourself using a reverse osmosis unit, which can be relatively costly.

- **Bottled water**, although it' is typically mineralized, it can also be suitable for adjusting water parameters. However, you must carefully select the right brands and read labels to ensure that the mineral content does not exceed 200 ppm (soft water). This alternative, while more expensive per liter than RO water is more suitable for emergencies (when the pet store is closed) or for nano aquariums (small volumes).

- **Rainwater** can also be considered for the mixing water. It is nearly as soft as RO water (KH = 0 and GH = 1°). However, it is not as pure due to the atmospheric pollution it may encounter before falling. This is particularly exacerbated in areas with high industrial activity. Despite this, it is not necessarily much more polluted than tap water and can be used in an aquarium if you have a convenient means of collecting it.

Water "recipe"

Recipe 1 : lower hardness (GH and KH)

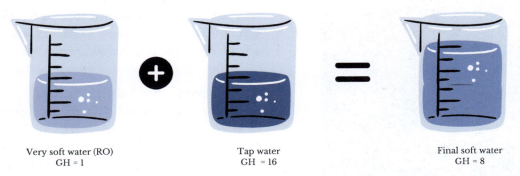

Very soft water (RO) GH = 1 + Tap water GH = 16 = Final soft water GH = 8

There isn't a precise recipe or formula for determining the quantities of water to mix based on the target hardness parameters. To achieve this, you'll need to perform successive tests until you reach the desired dosage. Nevertheless, it can be generally assumed that to reduce the hardness of water by half, you need to halve its mineral concentration. So, diluting 50 cl of water with a GH of 16 with an equal amount of water with a GH of 1 will yield approximately 1 liter of water with a GH of around 8. The same principle applies to minerals and nutrients but **not to pH** (as explained below).

For a 26 gal aquarium for example, you might need to prepare 13 gal of RO water mixed with 13 gal of tap water with a GH of 16 to obtain 26 gal of water with a GH of 8, which is suitable for most freshwater fish. Keep in mind that these adjustments should be made before introducing the fish.

Recipe 2 : Change the pH

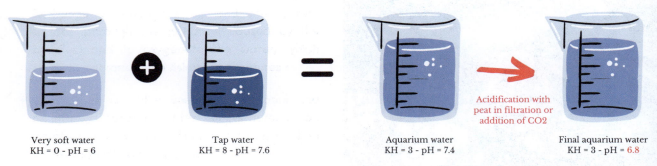

Very soft water KH = 0 - pH = 6 + Tap water KH = 8 - pH = 7.6 = Aquarium water KH = 3 - pH = 7.4 → Acidification with peat in filtration or addition of CO2 → Final aquarium water KH = 3 - pH = 6.8

It's also possible that the issue lies not with hardness or nitrates, but with a pH that is either too high (most commonly) or too low. In such cases, you'll need to address the KH first, lowering it to below 4°KH, and then acidify the water using various methods, such as peat filtration, CO_2 injection, or the addition of humic acids through the use of materials like catappa leaves, oak leaves, alder cones, and more.

BRINGING AN AQUARIUM TO LIFE

The nitrogen cycle

Continuing with our exploration of water, let's now delve into the essential and absolutely vital concept: the nitrogen cycle. Ammonia (NH3), nitrite (NO2), and nitrate (NO3) will be the main players in this chapter. We will demystify these somewhat complex chemical terms, understand their roles, and recognize their crucial significance for aquatic life.

A natural cycle

The trio of molecules - Ammonia, Nitrite, and Nitrate, all composed of nitrogen (N), forms the nitrogen cycle. This phenomenon is one of the most crucial concepts to understand and uphold in the realm of aquarium keeping.

If you've had some exposure to chemistry in your life, you might be familiar with the famous quote by the chemist Antoine Lavoisier :

"*Nothing is lost, nothing is created, everything is transformed.*"

The nitrogen cycle in aquariums is a principle that adheres word for word to this quote. It represents the natural biological process of breaking down various organic waste materials (fish excrement, leftover food, plant residues, carcasses, etc.) that progressively transform into different chemical substances under the influence of so-called aerobic bacteria (bacteria that require oxygen to thrive). These "good bacteria" are invaluable for their role in purifying the aquarium.

The waste materials first degrade into ammonia, which is quite toxic to fish, then into highly toxic nitrites at low concentrations, and finally into nitrates, which are less toxic and can be partly taken up by aquatic plants. In the absence of the beneficial bacteria, this cycle cannot be established, and the toxic substances cannot be broken down.

As a result, they accumulate in the water until reaching fatal concentrations for the fish.

Neglecting this cycle guarantees almost certain death for your fish and / or a detrimental long-term imbalance in your aquarium.

Start the cycle

In practical terms, to establish the nitrogen cycle and ensure a successful start to your aquarium, you need to run it under normal conditions but without any animals (no fish, shrimp, or snails).

After completing the setup (as recommended in the "Setting Up an Aquarium" section on page 51), you should activate all the technical equipment (keep the filter running 24/7, program the lighting for 7 hours a day, set the heater to the desired temperature) and let it run like this for a full month without any inhabitants.

During this period, beneficial bacteria will naturally develop in the tank and colonize all its parts, including the filter, substrate, and plants. These bacteria consume the initial pollutants, which mainly consist of decomposing plant material like dead leaves. It can also be helpful to add a small pinch of fish food to the water in the first few days to create additional pollution that stimulates bacterial growth.

Speeding up the cycle

An alternative technique is to artificially seed the aquarium with beneficial bacteria. This involves introducing these bacteria right from the initial setup through two different methods :

- You can take a portion of the filter media from a healthy, already cycled aquarium and place it in your own filter. This way, bacteria from the established aquarium will colonize your new tank.

- You can also purchase ready-to-use bacterial culture ampoules from pet stores. Generally, we're not big fans of this method as it offers no guarantees about the state or effectiveness of the contained bacteria. However, there are now some reliable brands available.

Both of these methods theoretically accelerate the cycling process for those who are impatient. But regardless of the method chosen, one step remains essential: regularly monitor your water parameters, especially nitrite levels, every two days during the first month. It's this parameter that will indicate when it's safe to introduce your fish, as it should spike before gradually approaching 0 ppm.

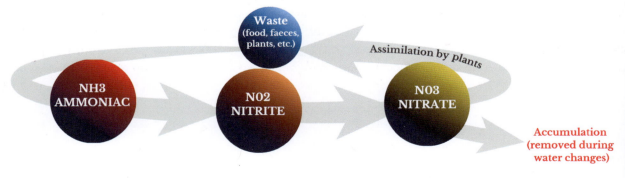

Nitrogen cycle in the aquarium : Under the action of various bacteria, waste materials transform into NH3 (ammonia), NH3 is then broken down into NO2 (nitrite), and NO2 is further converted into NO3 (nitrate). The nitrates are partially consumed by plants and algae, while the remaining nitrates accumulate in the water.

The nitrogen cycle

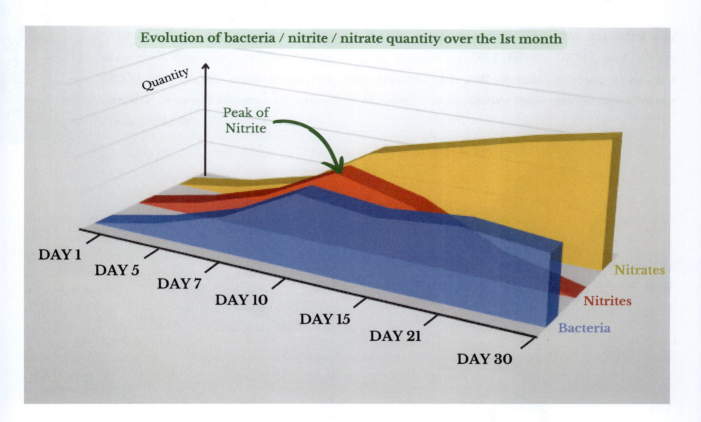

The graphic model above provides a chronological visualization of the nitrogen cycle during the first month of setting up the aquarium. Ammonia intentionally does not appear to avoid overloading the illustration. This graph highlights the simultaneous and proportional appearance of nitrites / nitrates and the bacteria responsible for waste nitrification. It shows that the quantities of bacteria, nitrites, and nitrates gradually increase between day 1, the day of setting up the aquarium with all its components (technical equipment, substrate, plants, etc.) and day 10 (variable duration). Day 10 marks the peak of nitrites, which is the moment when the nitrite concentration is at its highest.

Subsequently, the nitrite concentration will gradually decrease to reach 0 ppm around day 30 (still an approximate duration). This means that you can start introducing the first fish from day 30 onwards. The pollution generated by the fish can then be handled by the aerobic bacteria that have already colonized the tank during these first 30 days.

It's also worth noting that, unlike nitrites, nitrates do not decrease after day 10. As we'll see, there are no bacteria in the aquarium capable of breaking down nitrates into another substance. Therefore, without intervention in the form of water changes, the nitrate levels will continue to rise !

The nitrogen cycle

Ammonia

Ammonia is the substance directly produced by the organic waste introduced into the aquarium water (plant residues, fish excrement, leftover food, etc.). These waste materials are consumed and transformed into ammoniacal compounds by the initial types of bacteria, such as *bacillus sp* or *microcosus sp*. Depending on the water's pH, the final product of these microorganisms' action will be either ammonium (for pH < 7) or ammonia (for pH > 7). However, there is a notable difference between the two substances : while ammonium (NH_4^+) is slightly less toxic than ammonia (NH_3), it can be directly assimilated by plants unlike ammonia. This subtlety is especially important in certain types of aquariums, such as "low-tech" aquariums (without a filtration pump).

Furthermore, in an already cycled aquarium, the optimal amount of ammonia or ammonium should approach 0 ppm. A tolerance of up to 0.1 ppm may be acceptable, but you should then regularly monitor this value to ensure it doesn't increase. If it does, it means that the aquarium has either not been cycled correctly or that a significant imbalance has occurred, either killing the beneficial bacteria or overwhelming their purification capacity...

In the case of an excessive amount of ammonia (> 0.2 ppm), the ideal solution would be to restart the cycling process while removing the animals from the aquarium if possible. Otherwise, it's essential to urgently dilute the ammonia levels by performing significant water changes, approximately 50% every 2-3 days (while keeping the filtration system running continuously) and regularly testing the water parameters.

A sudden increase in ammonia levels can have various causes, such as overfeeding the fish, the presence of one or more decomposing corpses, overpopulation in the tank, deterioration of the biological filtration due to excessive cleaning of filter media, the use of chlorinated tap water with bactericidal properties, or an extended power outage that deprives the bacteria of oxygen.

High levels of ammonia first manifest as irritations in the form of burns on the gills and fins of the fish. These body parts may turn red to varying degrees, causing the fish to isolate themselves and/or remain immobile at the bottom of the tank. An excess production of mucus may then occur, indicating a weakening of the fish and be accompanied by respiratory distress, forcing the fish to gulp air at the water's surface.

The nitrogen cycle

Nitrites

Nitrites result from the oxidation of ammonia/ammonium by a second type of bacteria, known as *nitrosomonas sp*. Nitrites are highly toxic to fish, even more so than ammonia, even at low concentrations. Therefore, in a properly cycled and well-balanced aquarium, the nitrite levels should ideally be zero (0 ppm).

A tolerance of up to 0.05 ppm may be acceptable, but just like with ammonia, you should regularly monitor this value to ensure it doesn't increase further. When it exceeds 0.1 ppm, there is inevitably an imbalance in the aquarium that requires intervention.

First, you should mechanically reduce the nitrite level in the water by performing significant water changes of at least 30 to 40% every two days. Then, minimize nitrite production as much as possible by discontinuing feeding for a few days and then resuming feeding very sparingly. This way, the bacteria can develop at a rate proportional to the pollution and nitrite production.

The nitrite peak, well-known in aquarium keeping, refers to the more or less abrupt increase in nitrite levels in the aquarium water. Under normal circumstances and following the guidelines presented in this book, this spike occurs between one and two weeks after setting up the aquarium. It is entirely normal and reassuring for the future to observe it.

During this stage of the aquarium's life, there should be absolutely no animals inside (neither fish nor invertebrates).

The **complete disappearance of nitrites**, confirmed by tests, signals the green light for gradually adding fish to the aquarium.

Despite rigorously following these recommendations, an aquarium remains a delicate ecosystem, and you may still encounter a sudden increase in nitrites during its lifespan. You'll notice this through the behavior of the fish and should confirm it with a test.

A high level of nitrites in fish results in the destruction of hemoglobin, which makes up red blood cells. Since hemoglobin is responsible for oxygen transport, its reduction leads to respiratory difficulties, forcing the fish to stay near the water's surface to "gulp" air. If the nitrites are not quickly eliminated, the fish eventually dies from suffocation.

Nitrite levels

The nitrogen cycle

Nitrates

The final step in the nitrogen cycle involves the conversion of nitrites into nitrates, accomplished by a distinct group of bacteria known as *nitrobacters sp.* Fish exhibit considerably lower sensitivity to nitrates, which additionally contribute to the healthy growth of aquatic plants. Hence, it is advisable to maintain a sufficiently elevated nitrate level to uphold a harmonious biological balance. However, it's crucial to note that there is no natural nitrate removal process within an aquarium, leading to their inexorable accumulation over time, even in the presence of substantial vegetation. The sole means of reducing nitrate levels remains through water changes, underlining the integral role of water changes in aquarium maintenance, as we will delve into in the upcoming section.

An appropriate nitrate levels typically falls between 5 ppm and 15 ppm. Once it exceeds 30 ppm, heightened caution is warranted, as such concentrations can become toxic, particularly for highly sensitive invertebrates like shrimp, snails, and crayfish.

The production of nitrates is directly correlated with the population of animals in your aquarium. The more fish you have, especially larger ones, the greater the nitrate production, necessitating regular water changes. It's worth noting that the nitrate content in tap water can also vary, with some regions having tap water that is rich in nitrates.

Elevated nitrate levels can lead to various more or less problematic consequences. Once they exceed 50 ppm, nitrates begin to pose a toxicity risk to fish. Their circulatory system is the first to suffer, becoming irritated and weakened, resulting in fish becoming lethargic and more susceptible to diseases. Nitrates can also impede or even halt the fish's growth entirely.

A high nitrate concentration directly affects the aquarium's balance by promoting algae growth. In severe cases, with delayed intervention, algae proliferation can suffocate other life forms, both plant and bacterial, and facilitate the appearance of cyanobacteria. These cyanobacteria can further influence water parameters by causing a rapid increase in pH through biogenic decalcification.

This underscores the significance of regular water changes as the **sole dependable method** for reducing nitrate levels and maintaining a healthy aquatic environment for fish.

BRINGING AN AQUARIUM TO LIFE

Set up your 1st aquarium

Now that we've covered the theory, you possess all the knowledge needed to welcome and maintain your future aquatic residents in the best possible conditions.
So, let's put theory into practice!

Taking inventory

Before embarking on the task of setting up your aquarium, it's essential to take stock of all the components you have to ensure nothing is overlooked.

This checklist includes :

- The aquarium tank (with a lid if necessary)
- The filtration pump and its filter media
- The lighting system
- A heater with a thermostat (if required)
- Substrate(s)
- Decorative elements (such as roots, stones, etc.)
- Plants (naturals !)
- An aquarium thermometer
- A soft mat to place under the aquarium
- A multi-outlet power strip
- An plug-in Mechanical Timer

As for the work accessories, you'll need :

- A clean 3 us gal bucket (never used for chemicals)
- A sponge, absorbent paper or a mop
- Easily accessible water source
- A spray bottle for plants
- A flexible tubing
- A guide book (like the one you have now!)

Installation steps

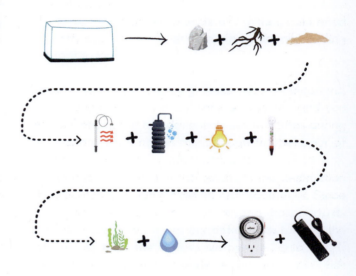

Aquarium : starter pack

Setting up step by step

 Time required to complete the example : 2h30

1 Cleaning and Rinsing

The first step involves cleaning the tank and the substrate (if necessary). To do this, pour a few millimeters of water into the bottom of the aquarium and use absorbent paper to gently scrub all the glass surfaces. **Do not use any detergent products**. To remove the water, you can either carefully lift and tilt the aquarium if its size allows (as in the case of a nano-aquarium) to pour out the contained water, or use a hose for siphoning or absorb it with a sponge.

This step serves to remove any potential residues (dust, remnants of silicone, etc.) and verify the integrity of the tank's seals. For larger tanks, try to make the best use of the cleaning water by using it to water your plants or wash your car.

Next, move on to cleaning the substrate. Nutrient-rich and specialized substrates should not be cleaned but placed directly in the aquarium. Other types of substrates, such as porous ones (like pumice) or neutral ones (such as Loire sand or quartz), should be meticulously cleaned and rinsed. Pour the substrate into a bucket or basin and cover it with clear water. Then vigorously rub it between your hands to remove as much dirt as possible. Discard the water and repeat this process until the water becomes clear.

Skip this step could result in a cloudy aquarium for several consecutive days after filling it with water, due to the substantial amounts of dust contained in these substrates which may become suspended when water is added. While this step may be somewhat time-consuming, it greatly contributes to the success of your aquarium setup.

Also, in parallel, it's advisable to boil natural decorative elements like stones and roots, if you have them, for approximately one hour.

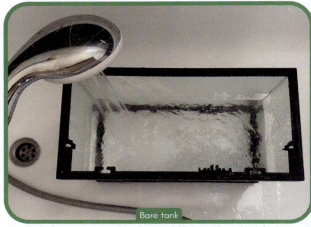
▲ *A shower jet is used to clean and fill the tank to check for leaks*

▲ *Rinse the neutral floor with clean water in a basin until the rinse water is clear.*

Set up your 1st aquarium

2 Setting up the Hardscape and Equipment

The second step involves placing the first layer of substrate and the initial decorative elements within the aquarium.

If you have envisioned a pronounced hardscape in your aquarium design (involving sizable stones and/or roots), it is preferable to position these directly against the back glass of the aquarium, even before adding the substrate. This approach is particularly important when dealing with species of digging fish that can undermine the decoration if it relies solely on the upper layers of the substrate.

If you have chosen to use porous and/or nutrient-rich substrates, follow the instructions in the "Additional Elements" section on page 23 to place these at the bottom of the aquarium. Afterward, position the hardscape elements by firmly embedding the stones into the substrate to prevent them from collapsing due to any substrate movement. Cover the underlayer with the previously cleaned and rinsed neutral substrate, spreading it to a sufficient depth, typically around 4 to 5 cm (1,5 to 2 inch).

Next, place the technical equipment (filter with filter media, heater, thermometer) in their final locations. To optimize their placement, choose their positions with future maintenance ease in mind. Additionally, try to position the heater and thermometer as close as possible to the filter outlet to ensure even heat distribution throughout the entire aquarium, facilitated by the water circulation generated by the filter.

Be careful not to connect any electrical equipment to the mains at this stage (except for lighting, if not too bulky, which will allow good visibility of the aquarium during planting).

▲ *Laying the 1st layer of substrate : in this case, lava rock granules*

▲ *Set up the hardscape by pressing the rocks into the substrate and gluing them in place to avoid any risk of rockfall. For difficult bonding, a piece of perlon soaked in glue can be used as a binder.*

▲ *Hardscape rendering after adding neutral soil*

Set up your 1st aquarium

3. Planting

Now comes the step that can be both the most satisfying and the most challenging! Before getting started, make sure to have certain tools on hand, including a pair of scissors, specialized aquarium tweezers, a plant mister, and, of course, a good amount of patience.

First, you need to remove the plants from their cultivation pots. There are two common configurations :

- Emerged cultivated plants and preserved in rock wool.
- In vitro-cultivated plants, often in nutrient gels.

For the first case, it's important to carefully extract the plant and its roots from the pot and the rock wool. It's not advisable to simply yank the plant out, as roots can become entangled in the pot, risking damage. Instead, a safer and more straightforward method is to use scissors to cut the pot along its height to split it open and then gently untangle any potentially stuck roots. Next, meticulously remove the rock wool, which serves as a root anchor. Again, be as gentle as possible to avoid damaging the roots. Trim the roots neatly with scissors (not your nails), leaving them at about 2 cm (0,8 inch) in length (which encourages better regrowth). A thorough rinse under warm, clear water will help remove any remaining residues.

For in vitro-cultivated plants, the procedure is simpler, requiring a thorough rinse under warm, clear water to remove as much of the gel as possible.

For the planting, two essential considerations must be taken into account. First, bury the roots sufficiently into the substrate for plants with roots to prevent any future uprooting. For epiphytic plants, secure or attach them using gel-type cyanoacrylate glue (there's no need to purchase specialized aquarium glues for this purpose; standard glues

▲ *All plants cleaned and prepared for planting*

▲ *The use of scissors enables roots to be cut cleanly, preventing them from rotting later on. (Don't use your nails !)*

▲ *Special aquarium pliers make planting easier by pinching the plant at its base and burying it deep in the soil without damaging it.*

Set up your 1st aquarium

available in any store are safe). Secondly, during the planting process, regularly mist the plants with water to prevent them from drying out, which could be detrimental to their well-being.

Stem plants are the most challenging to plant due to the absence of roots and rhizomes. One solution is to let them float at the water's surface. Many fish species appreciate this reassuring setup, as it provides shade and shelter for fry. However, it may not be the most aesthetically pleasing option and can potentially deprive other plants of light. The second approach is to plant them in the substrate after first securing the stems in a small "vase" (as illustrated here). This way, the stems will stay anchored in the substrate, forming a perfectly harmonious bouquet without the risk of rotting.

▲ Use a flexible silicone tube to wedge several stems. Remove the leaves along the entire length of the tube before inserting them into the tube.

▲ Regular spraying throughout the planting period prevents plants from drying out.

▲ Then plant the pipe serving as the plant's vase directly into the soil. Weight it down with a small stone to prevent future digging up.

Set up your 1st aquarium

◀ *Once the planting is complete*

4 Filling and Launching

At this stage, the most challenging part is usually behind you. However, extreme caution is required during this phase, as a momentary lapse of attention can undo all your efforts. It's essential to pay close attention to the water flow during the filling process, ensuring that it is not directed directly at fragile elements within the aquarium, especially the substrate, to avoid disturbing the entire setup.

To prevent this, you can, for instance, place a shallow dish at the bottom of the aquarium (or use your hand for smaller tanks), redirecting the water flow onto it to "break" the force of the flow.

As a result, the water will gradually flow to the bottom of the aquarium, filling it very gently. The water used should be the final water, with parameters suitable for the needs of the fish you plan to introduce into the tank. During the cycling process, water parameters may inevitably experience some variations that will need to be monitored and adjusted if necessary before adding the fish. It's important to note that during this period, and more generally throughout the life of the aquarium, the technical equipment (filter, heater, etc.) should never be turned off, except during maintenance.

If the water appears cloudy at the end of the aquarium filling, there's no need to worry. This cloudiness is often due to inadequate cleaning of the substrate or rocks but will typically dissipate within one or two days, thanks to the action of the filtration system.

▲ *In view of the small size of the aquarium used for this example, filling is done with a bottle of water. The jet is directed at the large central stone, breaking its force.*

Once filling is complete :

After the installation

Once the aquarium is completely filled, you can proceed to connect all the electrical equipment (pump, heater, and lighting on a timer).

For those using an external filter, it's crucial to note that, for most models, you must prime the suction by filling the pump with water before turning it on. Allowing air to be sucked into the filter can be detrimental to your equipment. Always refer to the user manual before undertaking any operation.

Next, you'll need to let the aquarium run in this manner for a minimum of one month to establish the nitrogen cycle. During this period, you (well, you!) will not be idle. After one week, it's time to commence with water parameter testing, particularly for nitrites, to detect their rise and peak. You can also perform tests for GH, pH, and KH to monitor the aquarium's progress, but they become especially significant before introducing fish and during the subsequent days/weeks to ensure everything is in order.

Actual maintenance will not take place during this conditioning phase, but you can perform some initial plant care by removing (and siphoning) any dead or excessively algae-covered leaves or plants.

Set up your 1st aquarium

Cycling monitoring

As mentioned, monitoring the nitrogen cycle is only possible through regular water testing. You can keep an eye on all three key parameters – ammonia, nitrites, and nitrates – if you desire (and your budget allows), but it's commonly recommended to focus on nitrites.

Starting on the 7th consecutive day after setting up the tank is a good baseline for testing. Afterward, testing every 2 days is sufficient to detect the rise and peak of nitrites.

When it comes to the duration and intensity of the cycle, there are no strict rules.

Every aquarium is unique, and as a result, the cycling processes and values observed can vary significantly from one tank to another. Some cycles may progress relatively quickly with pronounced spikes, reaching levels exceeding 5 ppm, while others may be more extended with spikes not exceeding 0.4 ppm, as was the case with our demonstration aquarium. The key is to meticulously monitor the progress to ensure that a peak has been surpassed before it diminishes.

Additionally, in the case of a minor spike, closely watch the nitrite levels again when introducing fish, as this can potentially trigger a second spike.

Monitoring of nitrite levels using drop tests

Day 7 : First test and first nitrite reading at 0.1 ppm.

Day 10 : Nitrite levels are rising, reaching 0.4 ppm.

Day 20 : Nitrite levels are down to an acceptable 0.025 ppm. Another week of testing will be carried out to validate this good value and allow the introduction of the first residents.

Set up your 1st aquarium

Fish introduction

It's done ! Your tank is finally cycled, and the nitrites have gone through a spike before dropping to 0 mg/l. Life has already begun to thrive in your aquatic world, with plants growing and harmless creatures like snails likely making an appearance along with the plants. Now it's time to introduce the first real inhabitants, but there are a few more precautions to take before doing so.

Before releasing (and even purchasing) any fish, you must (re)check the aquarium's water parameters. If you have the necessary tests (pH, GH, KH), that's a plus. Otherwise, bring a water sample (at least 10 ml) to a pet store that conducts tests with a liquid test kit, not test strips (usually free at most major pet stores). Always ask for the precise test values to verify that they align with the requirements of the fish species you intend to acquire. Don't settle for a simple "parameters are okay" from the seller. Once this final step is confirmed, you can finally purchase and bring home the eagerly anticipated new additions to the family.

The journey from the point of purchase to your home should be as quick as possible, ideally in the dark (prepare a opaque paper bag to place the bag containing the fish), and avoid sudden temperature fluctuations. Avoid undertaking this step on extremely hot or cold days. Upon arrival, you'll need to proceed with **acclimation**.

The acclimation of new arrivals is a two-step process. First, you'll perform acclimation to balance the temperature between the water in the aquarium and the water in the transport bag to prevent temperature shocks when releasing the fish. To do this, place the bag containing the fish directly in the aquarium water. The two waters will gradually equalize in temperature. Turn off the aquarium lights and wait for 15 to 20 minutes.

Once this time has passed, it's time for the "chemical" acclimation of the fish. This step aims to progressively balance the chemical parameters of the two waters, which can be quite different (pH, KH, GH, etc.). To do this, open the top of the bag with a pair of scissors (keeping it in the aquarium) and every 10 minutes, pour a small glass of water taken from the aquarium (approximately 10 ml). Repeat this process until the volume of water initially in the bag has doubled (approximately). Once this is achieved, use a net (or your hand) to catch the fish and release them into the aquarium.

Since the quality of the water in the transport bag is unknown, it is not recommended to pour it directly into the aquarium to avoid any risks.

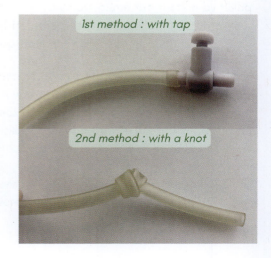

1st method : with tap

2nd method : with a knot

> ⓘ There is also a technique known as the drip acclimation, which allows for a slower and more gradual adjustment of water parameters. This method is especially recommended for invertebrates such as shrimp, which are more sensitive to fluctuations. It involves replacing the glass of water used to transfer aquarium water into the transport bag with a tube, with the flow rate set to approximately 2 drops per second, using a small valve or knot (see the photo provided). At this filling rate, it will take 1 to 2 hours for the water volume containing the shrimp to double or even triple.

Set up your 1st aquarium

For the KH test :

The vial initially contains 5 ml of water taken from the aquarium, and it turns blue after the addition of the first drop. You then continue to add the reactive solution drop by drop until the solution turns yellow. The number of drops added corresponds to the KH of the water.

For our aquarium, we added 9 drops, so our KH is 9.

For the GH test :

The same principle applies, with a red solution turning green after the addition of the reactive solution. The number of drops added corresponds to the °GH of the water.

For our aquarium, we added a total of 14 drops, so our GH is 14°GH.

For the pH test :

You use a control vial containing only aquarium water and a test vial containing aquarium water and 4 drops of the reactive solution. Wait for 3 minutes and compare the color of the solution obtained to the colors on the provided color chart.

For our aquarium, we obtained a pH of 7.3..

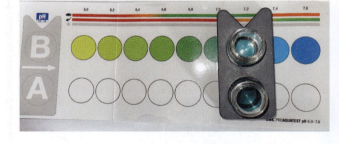

Next, you compare the water parameter results for your aquarium to the recommended parameters for the species you wish to introduce (in this case, CPO crayfish) to ensure compatibility. If the parameters do not match, you will need to perform water mixing to achieve the desired conditions.

Summary of how to set up an aquarium

1 Rinse the tank and check the seals for proper tightness.
Clean the substrate(s) with clear water until the water remains clear.

2 Place the first layer(s) of substrate at the bottom of the tank or position large stones directly against the back glass if burrowing fish will be present.
Cover with the final layer of substrate.

3 Finalize the hardscape, making sure everything stays in place (lightly tap with a finger to verify), and use cyanoacrylate gel glue if necessary.

4 Remove plants from their culture pots, rinse them, and plant them in the aquarium according to their type (roots in the substrate, rhizomes attached, or affixed to decorative elements).
Regularly spray with water to prevent drying out.

5 Set up the functional technical equipment (adjust the thermostat, insert filter media in the correct order, set the lighting on a timer, etc.) as per recommendations.
This part can also be done in step 3.
Fill the aquarium with water at the right parameters.

6 Test the water to monitor the establishment of the nitrogen cycle and the expected water parameters.
Introduce the fish following the acclimatization procedure.

✅ Enjoy observing your new aquatic world.

BRINGING AN AQUARIUM TO LIFE

Aquarium care

Depending on the size, equipment, and layout of your aquarium, the maintenance may vary, especially in terms of water change frequencies and volume. In all cases, it is crucial to keep your aquarium clean to ensure the well-being of your fish and to observe it carefully to adjust maintenance as needed.

Before any intervention in the aquarium, always disconnect electrical accessories (pump, heater, etc.) and wash your hands thoroughly with soap.

Water changes

Water changes play a crucial role in aquarium maintenance, serving two primary functions :

- Removing accumulated pollutants from the water, such as nitrates and phosphates.
- Replenishing essential trace elements consumed by plants and vital for invertebrates, like calcium and magnesium.

It's important to understand that an aquarium operates in a nearly closed system with limited interaction with the outside world, except for heat and food input. Unlike natural bodies of water that are regularly refreshed by the natural water cycle (runoff, rain, etc.), aquarium water remains unchanged if no human intervention takes place. While the biological nitrogen cycle purifies the water by removing toxic molecules, over time, it naturally depletes certain nutrients vital for plant growth. Conversely, it can accumulate other substances to concentrations that disrupt the aquarium's balance or even become lethal. Replacing some of the water with fresh water helps correct these imbalances.

To achieve these benefits, we recommend performing weekly water changes. Occasionally, the interval between water changes can be extended to two weeks or even up to a month, for example, during vacations, without harming the aquarium's health. In such cases, it's advisable to perform a slightly larger water change upon your return. **However, you should never change 100% of the aquarium water.**

Even a 50% change is rarely necessary except in urgent situations. For routine maintenance, changing a maximum of 10-15% of the water per week is recommended. The exact volume may vary depending on the state of your specific aquarium, which you'll assess through observations.

In a healthy, balanced aquarium without major issues (moderate algae growth, acceptable nitrite, nitrate, and phosphate levels, normal behavior of plants and fish, etc.), a 10% water change, roughly 2 us gal for an 20 us gal / 17 uk gal tank, should suffice. The percentage can increase to 20-50% only in cases of imminent danger to the fish (such as a sudden nitrite or nitrate spike due to pollution or illness) to restore stable water parameters (to be verified through water tests before and after the change).

The replacement water should have the same chemical composition as the aquarium water, with a temperature difference not exceeding 37°F. If tap water is used, it should be allowed to sit in an open container (e.g., water bottles, buckets, jerrycans) for 24 hours to allow chlorine to evaporate. You can also use a water conditioner product.

Aquarium care

The process of changing the water is relatively straightforward when you have the appropriate equipment. To do this, you will need :

- A clean container, such as a bucket, with sufficient capacity (at least 3 us gal).
- A siphon or a specialized aquarium vacuum, or a simple silicone filtration hose, with a minimum length of 1 meter (40 inch).
- A towel to dry your hands or any potential water spills outside of the aquarium or the container.

This operation is based on the siphoning technique and the difference in air pressure between one end of the hose (inside the aquarium) and the other end (positioned at a lower height in the container). By creating a vacuum, either by using your mouth (without swallowing!) or with a priming bulb pump, you will draw water from the aquarium and allow it to flow automatically into the container.

Here's an illustration of the process :

Siphoning with hose

End through which water is sucked

Depending on requirements, we can modify the equipment by adding for example, a valve to the hose, enabling control over the desired flow (the diameter of the hose determines the flow rate, and this can lead to overly rapid suction in smaller aquariums).

Additionally, we can equip the end of the hose inside the aquarium with a bell, facilitating simultaneous cleaning of the aquarium substrate.

Siphon to suck up waste from the aquarium floor

Valve can be connected to the hose to adapt the drain flow rate

Aquarium care

Substrate cleaning

Cleaning the substrate should be done on a weekly basis, coinciding with the water change. Using the suction hose, optionally equipped with a bell, it should facilitate the removal of larger debris scattered on the bottom. To prevent the inadvertent suction of sand, it's important to hover the bell approximately 5mm (0,2 inch) above the substrate. You can also use it to remove certain algae from plant leaves, specifically the green brush algae, or the viscous white mold that may develop on newly submerged roots.

Glass cleaning

Cleaning the aquarium glass should be carried out at varying intervals, depending on the specific conditions of your aquarium. Some tanks tend to accumulate a thin layer of green algae on their glass surfaces, which can hinder the enjoyment of observing the aquarium. For such cases, it is advisable to clean the glass daily using a magnetic algae cleaner (simple and efficient), a specialized aquarium scraper with a razor blade, or even a piece of cotton (less convenient, as it requires putting your hands in the water). *Please be mindful of gravel from the substrate that could get trapped between your cleaning tool and the glass during the process, potentially causing scratches.*

Stubborn white stains can also develop on your aquarium glass due to lime deposits. Just like in your bathroom, you can apply white vinegar to a cloth and gently rub the affected areas. Afterward, wipe it dry with a clean cloth, but exercise extreme caution to avoid spilling vinegar into the aquarium water.

Cleaning the decor

Cleaning the aquarium decor follows a similar approach to cleaning the substrate, where you use a hose to suction up various debris and algae that might have accumulated on the decorative elements. If you notice significant buildup, you can gently scrub the affected areas with a clean toothbrush, for example, before suctioning up the loosened residues.

Stubborn algae on plants can be removed by hand (by gently rubbing the leaves between your fingers), using a soft brush, or a small brush for filamentous algae. If the plant continues to be plagued by algae regularly, it may be necessary to trim the affected leaf or even the entire plant to completely eradicate the problematic algae.

▲ Magnetic glass cleaner for fast daily cleaning without disturbing aquarium life

No household or chemical cleaning products should be used in the maintenance of an aquarium. The sole cleanser, whenever possible, should be the used aquarium water (for rinsing filter media) or tap water for cleaning various accessories, excluding filter sponges.
All equipment used, such as buckets, hoses, and so on, should be designated exclusively for aquarium use to prevent any risk of contamination.

Filter cleaning

Filter maintenance is the most crucial aspect and must strictly adhere to certain guidelines, regardless of the type of filter you possess (internal, external, cascade, etc.).

First and foremost, **filter media should never be rinsed with tap water.** The chlorine present in tap water would kill off all the vital bacteria necessary for the nitrogen cycle, potentially leading to new spikes in ammonia or nitrites, which can be harmful.

Cleaning the filter media should coincide with one of your weekly water changes. With the old aquarium water you've removed, you can safely rinse the filter media in a bucket. It's not necessary for the media to look brand new when you place it back in the filter; just ensure that most of the debris is removed. You can then reassemble the filter in the aquarium and dispose of the dirty water (you can also use it to water your plants, which will appreciate this high-quality natural fertilizer!).

When the filter media appears significantly worn and overly porous (usually after several months), it will be time for replacement. However, another rule to follow: never replace all the filter media at once. You should only change half of the used foam blocks, cutting them in half and replacing one of the two halves. This way, the bacteria from the old foam will colonize the new one (the second half of the foam can be replaced the following week).

As for biological filter media (bio-rings, bio-balls, etc.), they should never be replaced. Simply rinse them with the drained aquarium water if too much dirt accumulates.

If you believe you've made a mistake in filter maintenance that could be detrimental to the survival of the beneficial bacteria, it's crucial to react promptly. To mitigate any potential harm, regularly test for nitrogenous compounds (ammonia, nitrites, and nitrates) and carry out significant water changes if necessary until acceptable levels are restored.

As for **the frequency of filter maintenance**, it will be highly variable and differ for each aquarium. Contrary to common misconceptions, more frequent maintenance is not necessarily better and could, in fact, disrupt the health of the bacteria and the biological balance of the tank. Filter maintenance should be performed when a need arises. This need can vary from every month, two months, six months, or even once a year (although less common).

However, this doesn't mean you should do nothing with your filter and wait for a complete blockage and issues to occur! A good practice is to visually inspect the condition of the filter media at least once a month. For some internal filters, a visual check from the outside may suffice, while others, like external filters with media contained in opaque containers, may require disassembly to access the media.

Based on the level of clogging, common sense will intuitively guide you on whether a rinse is necessary. If the filter media still appears sufficiently clean and porous, allowing water to pass through easily while removing waste, you can leave them in place until the next inspection. The strength of the filter's water output can also serve as a good indicator. If it has significantly decreased, it indicates that the filter has become significantly clogged and requires some cleaning.

Aquarium care

Maintenance schedule

	Checking equipment	Glass cleaning	Substrate and decor cleaning	Water change	Water tests	Plant care	Checking the filter
Everyday	🐟	🐟					
Once a week		🐟	🐟	🐟			
Every 2 weeks				🐟	🐟	🐟	
Every month							🐟

Regular and rigorous cleaning is the secret to the longevity of a healthy and perfectly balanced aquarium. And with the right equipment, cleaning will be all the easier and less painful.

Recommended maintenance equipment

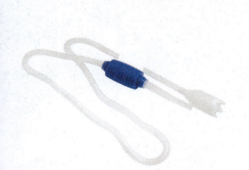

Water siphon with priming bulb

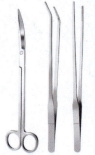

"Aquascaping" scissors and tweezers for trimming plants cleanly and planting them easily underwater.

Magnetic cleaner and algae scraper for glass

Two fish nets, adapted to the size of your aquarium

BRINGING AN AQUARIUM TO LIFE

Feeding your fish

Feeding your fish is, despite its outward simplicity, a delicate task in the world of aquarium care. It requires special attention, as it not only influences the well-being of your aquatic creatures but also directly affects the pollution level in your aquarium. Knowing how to feed your fish with the right foods and proper techniques is essential for maintaining the equilibrium of your tank. Let's explore these aspects in this section.

Type of food

There is a wide variety of products available today for feeding aquarium fish and invertebrates: dry, frozen, freeze-dried, live food, and more. There's something for every taste and, most importantly, for all types of fish. However, such diversity can be overwhelming when it comes to choosing the right food for your own fish.

The dietary regime of the inhabitants in your aquarium is the primary criterion to consider. Do you have any carnivorous, herbivorous, or omnivorous species? Each species indeed follows a specific dietary pattern that should be adhered to by providing them with nutritionally tailored food. Most aquarium species are omnivorous (likes Betta fish, Discus, Killifish, Ramirezi, Tetras, Corydoras, Gouramis, Rasboras and others). On the other hand, some rarer species are predominantly carnivorous, such as certain Neolamprologus species from the African lakes of Malawi and Tanganyika. Meanwhile, some tend to be more herbivorous, like Guppies, Platys, Mollies, or Loricariids such as Ancistrus and Otocinclus.

For the first two types, it's crucial to select food with a relatively high protein content for dry foods (exceeding 30%, typically indicating better product quality) and diversify with whole prey items, such as small crustaceans like artemia or daphnia, and insects like mosquito larvae or bloodworms, which can be provided in live, frozen, or even freeze-dried

forms. Conversely, for fish and invertebrates with herbivorous tendencies, it's essential to limit the intake of excessive proteins and favor foods rich in cellulose (plant fibers). Lastly, there are mixed composition products that are better suited for community aquariums, serving as a staple diet for the majority of fish.

The form of the food is the second factor to consider, especially when it comes to dry food. Flakes, pellets, sticks, or wafers - each form is better suited for certain species and their feeding habits, allowing them to feed near the water's surface (floating pellets, sticks, or flakes) or, conversely, in mid-water or at the bottom of the aquarium (sinking pellets or wafers). Size is also a crucial factor as it should be appropriate for the fish's mouth size. If the food is too large, the fish may not be able to swallow it and if it's too small, they might lose interest.

Furthermore, certain forms have advantages in terms of handling and dosage. For example, while flakes quickly disintegrate upon contact with water into numerous particles, pellets remain intact, preserving their nutritional quality and reducing the risk of water pollution (they are easier to retrieve in case of non-consumption).

The right gestures

When it comes to the right feeding practices for your fish, two key words should be at the forefront of your mind : variety and moderation.

A fundamental rule to follow is that it's better to underfeed your fish than to overfeed them. This is the number one mistake made by most beginners who tend to overfeed their fish out of fear that they might starve. Fish are true "gluttons," always ready to eat. It's essential to develop the right habits in response to this behavior, which means limiting feeding to once or twice a day and in small quantities (a common guideline is that all the food should be consumed within 2 minutes of being distributed). Ensure that all the fish have had access to the food, and remove any excess that hasn't been consumed within 10 minutes to prevent the risk of over-pollution. Fish can easily go several days without eating (typically 4 to 5 days), and it can even be beneficial for their health, especially when they reach adulthood, to fast them once a week. This helps them maintain a healthy weight and extend their lifespan.

Mealtime is also the perfect opportunity to observe your fish's behavior closely. If some of them refuse to eat, it may indicate inappropriate food (in which case, persist with a different type of food over several days) or, more critically, a health issue. A healthy appetite is generally a key indicator of a fish's well-being.

Another good practice is to maximize food variety by offering prey items (live or frozen) to omnivorous fish and vegetables (such as blanched zucchinis, carrots, spinach, or dried nettle leaves) to herbivorous fish and invertebrates at least once a month.

However, always make sure to research the potential toxicity of any food before introducing it into your aquarium.

▲ Always use your fingers to distribute the food in pinches, rather than pouring it over the water and shaking the can like a "salt shaker": this makes dosing much easier.

Feeding your fish

The various forms of dry food

Flakes

+ Suitable for fish with small superior mouth (turned upwards to catch food on the surface of the water). Once moistened, they soften, enabling even small fish to retrieve bits of the right size.

− Rapidly disintegrates in water, preventing total consumption and further pollution.
Difficult to dose and catch up with in case of "heavy hand".

Pellets

+ Whether "floating" or "sinking", with several different sizes, they adapt to all types of fish mouths. They stay in shape once in the water, allowing nutrients (especially vitamins) to be preserved and dosing to be made easier.

− Some fish do not appreciate this form of food.
Pellet size should be adapted to mouth size.

Sticks

+ As with pellets, they are available for all types of fish mouth, stay in shape once in the water and are easy to dose. Some fish will prefer colored sticks (e.g. red), which will mistake them for small bloodworms.

− Some fish do not appreciate this form of food (even in colored form). The size of the sticks should be adapted to the size of the mouth.

Wafers

+ Shape designed for bottom-feeding fish that sinks instantly to the ground once introduced into the water. It disintegrates very diffusely, leaving fish time to grate it with their mouths.

− Suitable only for bottom-dwelling fish such as Corydoras, Loricaridae or invertebrates.

Freeze-dried prey

+ Wide variety of prey (insects such as mud worms, tubifex or crustaceans such as artemia, daphnia, crisp, ...) to vary the diet while offering a much longer shelf life than live versions.

− Suitable only for carnivorous or omnivorous fish.
To be used occasionally (once or twice a week maximum) as a supplement to a basic food consisting of flakes, granules or sticks.

COMMON PROBLEMS AND SOLUTIONS

COMMON PROBLEMS AND SOLUTIONS

Water parameters problems

The drift in aquarium parameters stands as the most prevalent and paramount cause of an array of issues, ranging from a mere algal overgrowth to the demise of both fish and the aquarium itself. Diligent maintenance and meticulous observation of the tank typically serve to detect any anomalies. However, it is often at the water parameters level where intervention will be required to resolve the issue and prevent any recurrence.

Algae

Every aquarium enthusiast, no matter how experienced and meticulous, will inevitably encounter algae in their aquarium at some point. Like puberty and acne, algae are an unavoidable phase in the life and maturation of an aquarium. They are not a problem in themselves, but can become problematic when beginners allow them to proliferate uncontrollably.

Algae are nothing more than a species belonging to the plant kingdom, just like the aquatic plants in the aquarium. Although they function slightly differently and are much more resilient, giving them a distinct advantage over their plant cousins, they still have the same basic needs: light and carbon dioxide for photosynthesis, and nutrients such as nitrates, phosphates, and minerals to grow and multiply. An aquarium where algae thrive is, therefore, an aquarium where plants thrive much less, and the former take advantage of the latter's weakness.

So **the battle against algae** primarily begins with... better care of the plants. Not very intuitive, but ultimately quite logical, wouldn't you agree ?

We forget steer clear of harmful anti-algae products (harmful not only to algae but also to the aquarium ecosystem), costly purchases of a variety of cutting-edge products and equipment (though some can be beneficial in specific situations - we will revisit this later), and all those dubious pieces of advice aiming to provide purely curative solutions, rarely addressing the root of the problem. But so, what should you do?

First and foremost, revisit, if necessary, the section on "Plant Needs" on page 30 to understand how to cultivate robust, beautiful plants capable of suppressing algae formation. Of course, it's not always so straightforward. Despite all the right practices and habits adopted for proper plant maintenance, you may still, almost inevitably, find yourself grappling with these troublesome algae. In such cases, you'll need to identify and directly address the root cause(s) of the issue. But how do you determine it in this scenario ? Is it inadequate lighting ? Is there not enough CO2 in the water (or too much in the case of injection) ? Are nitrates or phosphates at excessive levels? Do your plants require more nutrients? Is it a combination of several of these factors ? As we have seen, numerous factors influence plant growth, and thus, multiple factors can explain the emergence of algae.

Slowly but surely

Slowly not in the swiftness of action, which should not wait, but in the potential multitude of actions that could prove counterproductive.

Firstly, it is vital to meticulously observe the progress of your aquarium on a daily basis. This is the most effective way to detect any issues as early as possible. When the first signs of algae are thus spotted, it is essential to plan an imminent maintenance session to promptly remove them, thereby slowing their growth and identifying the initial adjustment to be made (such as reducing the lighting duration if it's excessively long).

However, discretion is the better part of valour. You should always allow the modification you've just implemented to take effect and proceed step by step. In the realm of science, we would refer to this as an iterative method. Let's consider a specific scenario: Your aquarium has completed its cycle, and shortly after introducing the first fish, green algae have also made an appearance... Quite unfortunate ! The proposed iterative method urges us to identify the initial potential cause of these algae and provide an initial solution.

It becomes apparent that the irregular lighting in your aquarium, resulting from the absence of a timer and manual switching on and off at occasionally random hours, is the issue. To address this, you decide to implement an initial correction by automatically programming the lights for 7 hours a day. Following this adjustment, you exercise **patience for several weeks** (a minimum of 4 or 5 weeks) to allow the aquarium and its inhabitants to respond and adapt to this new setting. Remember, we are essentially "playing" as amateur chemists, attempting to recreate nature in our aquarium and nature requires time. Once this period has passed, and if there is no noticeable improvement in the situation, you can conclude that the isolated factor (in this case, the lighting rhythm) was not the primary cause of our problem. You can then proceed with a second action, following the same pattern (for instance, reducing the lighting duration this time).

All too often, we witness inappropriate problem resolutions carried out due to either a lack of knowledge (or following poor advice) or impatience and a desire for quick fixes. It is common to see novice aquarists resort to using an anti-algae product as their initial course of action in an aquarium with a still-fragile balance. While such products can be effective in a curative sense, they never address the root cause, which will inevitably resurface, possibly with greater intensity. Let's continue with our hypothetical experiment.

The anti-algae treatment will indeed eliminate a substantial portion of the algae, but it will also weaken the plants (which, like algae, are also vegetation). Remember, healthy and robust plants are the best defense against algae through competition for the same nutrients in a shared environment. Furthermore, algae are more resilient and responsive than plants, so they will rebound in the event of a new issue (which isn't really new, as the root cause of the initial algae problem hasn't been resolved), outcompeting the plants. If you're brave, you may not give up right away, attempting various other maneuvers to rejuvenate your plants (such as adding CO_2, fertilizers, changing the lighting system, etc.), but in vain - except for the joy of... the now stronger algae. We don't want to reach that point !

Therefore, let's embrace this tried-and-true method, approved by many aquarists: maintaining an aquarium with lush vegetation and ensuring the healthiest possible plants !

Summary of algae control procedure

1. Testing your water parameters, especially nitrate, phosphate, and potentially silicate levels (ideal nitrate levels should range between 25 ppm and 50 ppm, while phosphate should be maintained between 0.02 and 0.1 ppm). Subsequently, perform a preventive water change slightly larger than usual (around 20 to 30%), ensuring the removal of as many algae as possible.
Ensure regular and meticulous tank maintenance (prompt algae removal upon their appearance, weekly water checks and changes, appropriate and non-excessive feeding, well-functioning filtration, etc.).

2. Next, proceed iteratively if no improvement is observed by implementing one correction at a time (reduce lighting duration, then introduce CO2, followed by fertilization, and so forth). Multiple simultaneous actions can sometimes have the opposite effect of what is intended.

3. Allow sufficient time after each action affecting the aquarium's operation (such as changing lighting duration, adjusting fertilizer doses, CO2 levels, etc.). Both algae and plants do not react immediately to changes; they require an adaptation period. Not being patient means having no insight into the actions taken and their results.

4. Incorporate fast-growing plants to compete with algae proliferation, such as Ceratophyllum Demersum or Elodea (refer to plant profiles for suitable options).

5. In case of a worsening situation, and as a curative measure, employ direct combat tools (UV filters, inhibitor, snails, etc.) against algae while concurrently investigating and rectifying the root cause of proliferation. For algae-eating organisms, always ensure they have sufficient food once the algae are removed.

Parameters problems

Common algae varieties

◀ Green algae

Green algae spread across all elements of the aquarium, including plants, glass, substrate, and decorations, in the form of tiny, velvety green filaments or hard patches. They proliferate rapidly in an unbalanced tank (excessive light, excessive nutrients, etc.). Nevertheless, green algae are an indicator of the aquarium's overall health and typically require only minor adjustments to eliminate them.

◀ Brown diatom algae

Brown diatom algae are recognized by the development of a brown/rusty-colored layer on plants, stones, or the substrate. Their growth is encouraged by inadequate lighting and elevated silicate or ammonia levels in the water. However, it is normal to observe them during the initial weeks of cycling a new aquarium. They should rapidly disappear once the aquarium has reached a stable equilibrium.

◀ Red algae

Red algae encompass various types of algae such as Black Beard Algae or Staghorn algae. They are some of the most resilient algae to eliminate in an aquarium. They can be identified by their appearance: small tufts for brush algae and dense filaments for staghorn algae. However, they are typically black/gray with blue-gray reflections rather than truly red, as their name suggests.

They can develop on virtually all elements of the aquarium, including plants, substrate, glass, decorations, as well as technical components like the filter or heater. They attach firmly and are not consumed by any aquatic animals. The only way to address them is by manual removal (using a brush and scraper for the glass and by siphoning all particles to prevent their dissemination, thereby encouraging their spread), and by trimming the leaves of affected plants.

Like other algae, they appear due to an imbalance in the tank, but their growth seems to be favored by warm and alkaline water conditions (pH above 7) and/or strong water circulation

◀ Cyanobacteria (Blue-Green Algae)

Cyanobacteria, or blue-green algae, is a hybrid between algae and bacteria. This type of bacteria possesses the unique ability to utilize photosynthesis for energy production, which is why it is often associated with algae. It can be identified by its slimy texture, vibrant color (ranging from green-blue to red), and its distinct unpleasant odor. It tends to thrive in areas of stagnant water. Highly prolific, it should be removed promptly upon its appearance and whenever detected. It can be easily removed through siphoning. While not harmful to fish, as they do not consume it, it can be toxic to humans and pets (dogs, cats, etc.) if ingested.

Parameters problems

Anti-algae accessories

Far from being essential, some accessories designed to limit the appearance or proliferation of algae can, in certain cases, prove effective. The major drawback of the equipment presented below is their considerable cost for limited usage. However, some individuals may find them beneficial and it is good to be aware of these options.

The UV filter is a remarkably effective accessory in the case of pre-existing algae issues, resulting in greenish water (caused by the suspension of microscopic green algae that are impossible to remove manually). This phenomenon, harmless to fish, can occur abruptly and be quite bewildering, often with no readily apparent warning signs.

In conjunction with investigating the root cause (lighting, water parameters, etc.), a UV filter can be used to eliminate the existing algae, swiftly restoring clear water. This filter is a module consisting of a sealed, opaque frame containing a UV-C lamp (ultraviolet of type C). This type of radiation has algaecidal properties as well as bactericidal and germicidal effects. Therefore, it can also be used in cases of disease, for example, to disinfect and sterilize the aquarium water. The advantage of this equipment is that it only affects the water and its components. It should be connected to the outflow of an external filter, ensuring it never comes into contact with the beneficial bacteria in the aquarium, as well as the plants and fish. Some models come with an integrated water pump to avoid the need for an additional external filter purchase if you do not already have one (UV filters are incompatible with all types of internal filters).

▲ A derelict aquarium, with green algae water

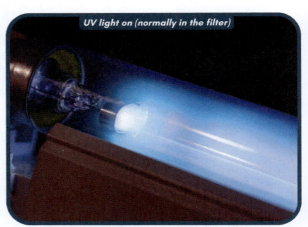
▲ Example of a UV-C lamp - never look into the naked eye

Parameters problems

Algae inhibitor, based on the principle of electrolysis, have the same objective and are increasingly found in aquariums. They are simpler to use and are often favored for their design appeal. However, they are quite effective under the condition that they are installed when setting up the aquarium initially. Otherwise, they will have little to no curative effect on algae.

In addition to being relatively costly (around 100$ / 80£ at the time of writing this book), the products available on the market may not always justify their price in terms of quality, particularly with a potentially limited lifespan (less than a year). It's worth noting that when used in hard water, the reactor (the submerged part containing the grids serving as electrodes) can become fouled more quickly, reducing the system's performance. Soaking it in a solution of white vinegar (or lemon juice) for a few hours, followed by a scrub with a toothbrush, facilitates effective cleaning. Beyond a certain range of water conductivity, the system may not function at all.

Algae-eating fish such as the Siamese Algae Eater, Bristlenose Pleco, Otocinclus, as well as shrimp and snails like ramshorn snails, also serve as valuable cleaning aides against algae. However, even though their contribution in the battle against algae invasion can be significant, one should not place all their hopes in them or regard them as mere maintenance accessories. They should be treated as full-fledged inhabitants of the tank with their own needs to meet (and the pollution they generate). Therefore, they should be factored into the total population calculation concerning the aquarium volume.

Algae Inhibitor off

Water sterilizer running

Algae-eating fish

Diseases

Preventing, recognizing, and treating the main diseases of your scaly residents is one of the many essential skills to possess as an aquarist. In this chapter, we will explore how to manage these less pleasant aspects of this hobby and, most importantly, how to minimize their occurrence. Generally, once a disease takes hold, it progresses rapidly and can lead to the death of a fish or even the entire population.

Common causes

Diseases encountered in the aquarium often share common causes. Being able to anticipate these causes to prevent diseases is the first step in the fight against them. Not surprisingly, the most common cause is poor maintenance conditions: inappropriate water parameters for the species (temperature, nitrites, nitrates, pH, etc.), inadequate nutrition (quality, variety, etc.), and stress (insufficient hiding places, limited swimming space, etc.). These factors can result from your own actions or the previous owner's maintenance practices. They weaken the fish's immune system, making it less effective against naturally occurring external threats.

The other primary cause is the direct introduction of a pathogenic agent into the aquarium (viruses, bacteria, fungi, molds, etc.). This is why it is essential to thoroughly clean any external elements (roots, stones, decorations, hands, etc.) and to establish quarantine in an isolated tank for plants and other new living organisms introduced later (fish, shrimp, snails, etc.).

Warning signs

Any behavioral or physical changes in your fish should raise a red flag. The signs of a problem are quite common, and here is a non-exhaustive list of symptoms to be alert to:

- Loss of appetite or regurgitation of food
- Difficulty in swimming, floating at the surface, or assuming a vertical position
- A fish appearing lethargic, resting on a decoration or at the bottom of the aquarium
- Physical abnormalities (swollen abdomen, torn fins, white spots, etc.)
- White, stringy feces adhering to the anus.

These observations are crucial, **especially before acquiring fish** (exercise particular caution when purchasing from pet stores). Furthermore, it is important to pay attention to even the slightest symptoms that will help precisely identify the fish's illness and, consequently, treat it effectively without risking further harm with an inappropriate treatment.

Diseases

Good habits

There are numerous diseases, some more common than others. However, it's crucial to remember that when it comes to fish, it's decidedly more challenging to treat a declared disease than to prevent it. That's why impeccable maintenance and vigilant, regular observation of the aquarium stand as your best tools in the fight against diseases.

When faced with a confirmed case of illness, the key is to react as swiftly as possible. Firstly, to optimize the chances of survival for the affected fish. Secondly, to minimize the spread throughout the entire tank. To achieve this, two essential steps come to the fore : testing and isolating.
Examining the water and its various parameters offers an initial clue to the underlying issue. If the test results appear satisfactory, then a more in-depth investigation is in order. If the case is isolated (affecting only one or a few individuals), a swift quarantine is necessary.

The hospital tank is indispensable for this purpose. In theory, any container with a lid can serve, as long as it has a capacity of 3 to 4 us gal. This could be a nano-aquarium if you already possess one, or a simple food-grade opaque plastic box to mitigate any risks.

This container should remain bare, **devoid of any equipment** except for a small 25W heater with a thermostat and optionally an air pump. Without lighting, filtration, or substrate (for easier cleaning), it won't be cycled and will necessitate regular water changes (50% every 2-3 days) to prevent pollution peak.
Nonetheless, it's important to exercise moderation by providing very light or even no feeding at all to the fish in the hospital tank. Any excess food that goes uneaten should be promptly removed.

The hospital tank should not be kept constantly filled with water. Instead, it should serve as a temporary holding tank for new fish or plants, allowing them to undergo a quarantine period. Additionally, it's essential for isolating sick fish and administering treatments.

Once the treatment or quarantine period for the fish is complete (at least 15 days), and there are no signs of illness, you can safely transfer your fish from the hospital tank to the main aquarium. Afterward, you'll need to thoroughly empty the hospital tank and disinfect all elements (the tank and accessories) that have been in contact with the sick fish using a bleach solution. Rinse everything meticulously with fresh water, and store the tank until its next use.

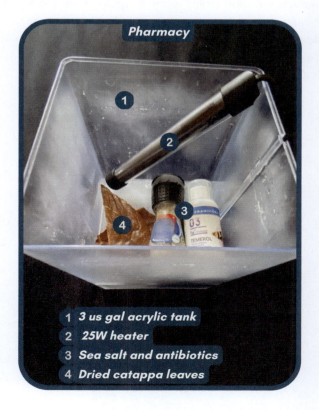

Pharmacy
1. 3 us gal acrylic tank
2. 25W heater
3. Sea salt and antibiotics
4. Dried catappa leaves

Table salt treatment

The use of table salt (sodium chloride), or a salt bath, can be an intriguing curative option for various fish ailments and diseases, serving as an alternative to medicinal treatments. Salt indeed offers several advantages for aquarium applications, provided it is used judiciously and with the right type of salt. Its antiseptic properties, facilitated through osmotic processes, make it effective against bacterial, fungal, and parasitic infections such as ich, oodinium, and fungal infections.

Furthermore, the ready availability of salt in every shop, its cost-low and its indefinite shelf life render it a valuable asset in our fish pharmacy.

However, despite its natural origins, there are precautions to be observed when using salt. Firstly, not all commercially available salts are suitable for aquarium use. It is imperative to select salt that is composed of 100% pure sodium chloride. Many table salts contain undesirable additives like fluoride or iodine to avoid.

Secondly, the impact of salt can be detrimental to living organisms if dosed improperly (overdosed). Some species are so sensitive to its effects that it's advisable to avoid treating them with salt, including plants, invertebrates (shrimp, snails, etc.), and certain scaleless fish (corydoras, loaches, loricariids, kuhlis, etc.), as they may not tolerate the salt treatment. For other fish, the treatment should ideally be administered in isolation, within a hospital tank.

How to use salt ?

Salt treatment is a comprehensive curative approach and should be treated with the same level of caution as medication. Never combine salt treatment with other parallel medicinal treatments. Depending on the fish's condition and the specific pathology, different salt treatments are viable, such as the light bath and the high-concentration bath.

The light bath serves as the fundamental treatment, involving the fish in water with a low salt concentration for a variable duration. This treatment is effective against mild to moderate bacterial and fungal infections, as well as some cases of constipation or indigestion. It may, however, be ineffective in advanced disease stages. To execute this treatment, prepare the water by diluting 20 grams of salt in 1 us gal of water or 5g / liter (approximately 1 teaspoon). Submerge the fish and leave it until signs of improvement are observed (a variable duration, up to 10 days). Change the water every day or every two days, replacing 50% of the salted water with fresh, unsalted water. Wait for a few more days (5 to 7 days) and return the fish to its aquarium if a complete recovery is observed.

High-concentration baths involve briefly immersing the sick fish (no more than 10 to 15 minutes) in water with a high salt concentration, at a rate of 100 g / us gal or 25g / liter, inducing an osmotic shock. This technique is considerably more aggressive for the fish, especially its mucus layer. Gradual desalination of the water and acclimatization are mandatory before reintroducing the fish to the aquarium (using a drip system over a period of 1 hour). High-concentration baths are more effective in combatting parasitic diseases. If the fish exhibits abnormal behavior during the bath, such as erratic swimming or being on its back, it must be promptly removed.

Changing an aquarium element

Substrate, filtration system, plants, decorations - an aquarium is a living ecosystem that evolves and matures. However, it is also a world that should continue to visually delight its owner to remain a source of pleasure. In this context, it may become necessary to make a few modifications, some of which are more straightforward to implement than others. In this section, we will explore the changes that can be easily made, as well as those that require a more complex approach, along with the proper methodology to avoid any potential issues.

Filtration system

The filtration system is the true heart of the aquarium, and changing it can have dramatic consequences if not done correctly. Therefore, it's essential to avoid replacing this component as much as possible and only do so in the case of technical issues (electrical failure, malfunctioning suction pump, external filter leakage, etc.).

Another (bad) reason for changing the filter might be an initial miscalculation of its size (filtration capacity) concerning the current aquarium population and the pollution generated. To prevent finding oneself in this situation, following the advice provided throughout this guide should suffice !

To proceed with the replacement of the pump/filtration system, the first step is to ensure the compatibility of the new equipment with the existing aquarium, especially in terms of size (ensuring sufficient space in the aquarium for an internal filter or adequate storage space for an external filter).

Lhe replacement procedure is not complicated, but it hinges on one crucial point : recovering the old biological filter media and incorporating them into the new filtration system.

It's possible that the configurations of the two filters are entirely different, requiring some adjustment in the size or shape of the old filter media, such as the foam. For solid filtering materials like ceramic noodles or sintered glass, you can place and mix them directly with the new ones if they are provided.

If the two filters are too dissimilar to allow any adaptation of the old filter media, you will need to manually recover as many beneficial bacteria as possible. To do this, you should prepare a container of at least 3 us gal that has never contained any chemical or household products. Fill it halfway with aquarium water, then place all the filter media inside to "rinse" them of their beneficial bacteria. The water in the container, now enriched with these beneficial bacteria, should be collected and poured into the filter (if it's an external filter) or directly into the aquarium with the new filtration system already running. This way, the recovered bacteria will quickly colonize the new filter and start thriving.

Nevertheless, it's important to monitor the ammonia and nitrite levels in the days following the filter replacement by conducting water tests.

Plants and decorations

Replacing plants and decorations is the least risky operation for the aquarium. Its level of delicacy will naturally depend on the extent of the intended modification (redoing the entire layout might be more complex than removing a single plant), but there are no specific rules to follow. For plants with extensive root systems (such as hygrophilas, cryptocorynes, echinodorus, etc.), it is advisable not to completely uproot them. Instead, extract only the above-ground part of the plant and trim the roots with a pair of scissors, avoiding disturbing the entire substrate.

Be cautious during these manipulations to avoid unintentionally harming or removing any of your aquarium's inhabitants (shrimp, for instance, can easily be overlooked in a dense clump of plants). To prevent this, always place the elements removed from the aquarium in a container filled with a bit of aquarium water, allowing you to check at the end of the operation that no animals are present.

The soil

Changing the substrate is the most time-consuming and labor-intensive operation to perform, as it involves nothing less than completely emptying the aquarium of all its elements. The motivation for changing the substrate can vary, whether it's the desire to have a substrate more suitable for plant growth (such as a technical substrate or one with nutrient-rich components) to facilitate the cultivation of more intricate plants (like carpeting plants or colorful varieties), or simply to give your aquarium a fresh look (such as transitioning from a light-colored substrate to a dark black one).

The procedure for changing the substrate will be nearly the same as for setting up a new aquarium, with a few additional precautions :

- Siphon and store the aquarium water in suitable containers (bottles, buckets, jerrycans, etc.).

- Isolate the fish, invertebrates, and plants in temporary containers (hospital tank, Tupperware, buckets, etc.).

- Remove technical components (heater, filters, thermometer, etc.) as well as decorative elements (rocks, driftwood, etc.). Keep the filter connected and submerged in the aquarium water to ensure the bacteria it houses continue to receive oxygen.

- Once the aquarium is completely emptied, proceed to remove the old substrate. You can use a small gardening shovel or a scoop, depending on the size of your tank. Rinse the tank thoroughly to remove any remaining debris.

- Then, place your new substrate and set up the aquarium according to the method outlined in the chapter "Setting Up Your First Aquarium" on page 51.

- Re-fill the tank with the initial water, reconnect the technical components, and reintroduce the inhabitants (no need for acclimation if the temperature in the containers holding the fish is similar to that of the aquarium).

- Top up with water with parameters matching those of the aquarium if necessary.

This is the only method for completely changing the substrate of your aquarium. Allow for half a day (for a 5 to 20 us gal aquarium) to two full days (or more) for a larger tank. During this period (3 to 4 days), the fish can safely stay in their temporary containers. Do not feed them to avoid the risk of pollution and monitor the temperature of their water.

DIFFERENT TYPES OF AQUARIUM

Which aquarium to choose ?

Various types of aquariums can be created, depending on the aquarist's level of experience and expectations. In this section, we will explore different categories of aquariums, ranging from community or beginner-specific aquariums to more complex setups like biotope and aquascape tanks, as well as the popular nano aquariums.

The type of aquarium you choose should align with your expectations regarding the desired final result. Were you drawn to the world of aquariums because you have a particular species in mind, or is it simply the idea of owning an aquarium that interests you? This single question already helps refine several other criteria, offering two possible configurations: an aquarium designed around the desired fish or an aquarium designed with a specific final layout in mind. Before acquiring any fish (or other components), it's important to keep in mind the type of aquarium you envision.

You can opt for a community tank if you want to house various species of different fish, or a species-specific tank with only one species to accommodate their specific temperament and perhaps encourage breeding. If the layout and aesthetic presentation take precedence, you may explore nano aquariums, which are suitable for small living spaces, biotope aquariums that closely replicate natural ecosystems from different parts of the world, or aquascape-style aquariums that showcase creatively designed landscapes, such as a forest or mountain range.

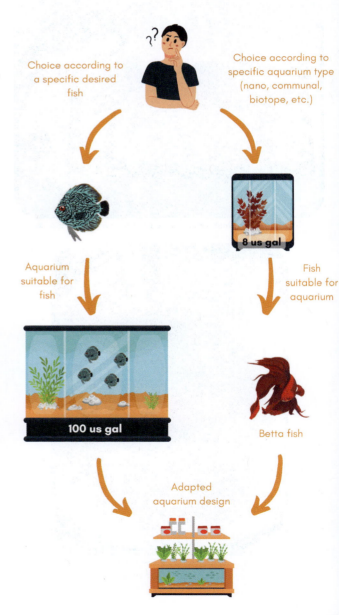

ACCORDING TO THE FISH

The community aquarium

The community aquarium is the most common type of aquarium and often preferred by beginners who are eager to have a variety of fish with different appearances, colors, and behaviors. However, it's not necessarily the easiest to maintain, nor is it the one we recommend most for beginners. If you opt for a community aquarium, it's essential to follow the recommendations that follow to ensure the success of your project !

Populating the aquarium

The key point once again lies in the desired type of fish : it is essential, especially for a community aquarium, to pre-determine the fish species you wish to maintain in your tank and their total number in the long run. The primary concern here is succumbing to irresistible purchases, often referred to as "impulse buys," which can lead to an imbalanced aquarium, resulting in algae overgrowth, diseases, fish fatalities, and potentially jeopardizing your budding passion. Conducting thorough research, species by species, will enable you to assess the feasibility of your aquarium. To do this, you'll need to ask yourself a series of questions during your research.

- Does the size of the aquarium provide a volume suitable for the adult size of the desired fish species and their quantity ? (Some fish are social and require a minimum of 10 individuals to form a school.)
- Is the future cohabitation of the various envisioned species feasible ? (Considering territory, behavior, etc.)
- Are the swimming locations of each species compatible ? Some species prefer the bottom, while others inhabit the surface or midwater. Overcrowding in a particular area of the aquarium with multiple species can stress the inhabitants and lead to competition. Ideally, one species per designated zone is recommended.
- Are there any species that interact with plants ? Some species may feed on or constantly uproot plants while foraging in the substrate. In such cases, planting the tank may not be possible.
- Do the water parameter requirements align ? (Each species may have differing needs in terms of pH, GH, temperature, etc.)

To address each of these questions for every species you consider acquiring, it's essential to conduct comprehensive research. You can certainly make use of the information available in books that provides insights into various species or on the web. Once you have identified potential species, the next step is to ensure their compatibility in terms of cohabitation.

Fishes

Once you have thoroughly established your plan for a community aquarium, which includes carefully selecting the appropriate fish species and determining their final quantity in accordance with your tank's size and layout, it is essential to adhere to a vital rule: the gradual and controlled introduction of fish into your freshly prepared aquarium. This advice is universally applicable to any type of aquarium, but it holds particular significance for community aquariums, where the enthusiasm for acquiring a multitude of fish can be overwhelming.

The initial reason for this gradual introduction is to allow the nitrogen cycle to adapt optimally to the new pollution generated. As we've discussed, beneficial bacteria develop in response to pollution levels. However, this development is not instantaneous but requires a certain period of adaptation. In the event of an excessive introduction of fish and, consequently, a rapid increase in pollution, the nitrogen cycle may become disrupted, potentially resulting in dangerously elevated nitrogenous compounds (ammonia, nitrites, nitrates). Furthermore, introducing fish gradually allows novice aquarists to acclimate themselves gently to the various responsibilities and challenges associated with maintaining an aquarium. In the event of issues arising from inadvertent actions, handling errors, accidents, or lack of knowledge, the consequences are likely to be less severe in a sparsely populated aquarium with greater resilience than in a fully stocked tank operating at its capacity limit.

In general, it is advisable to begin with a small school of the same species of fish (with a number suitable for the gregarious nature of the species), which can be gradually supplemented every 1 to 2 months with a new species. To determine the maximum number of individuals (valid for smaller species only), a guideline is to allocate 0,3 US gal of water per 1 cm of <u>adult fish</u>. For example, if a fish reaches a size of 3 cm as an adult, you can introduce a maximum of 20 individuals into a 18 US gal tank that is properly filtered and planted (20 x 3 cm x 0,3 gal = 18 gal).

Disadvantages of community aquariums

As you've likely discerned, the pitfalls of a community aquarium for a beginner lie in how swiftly the biological capacities of the tank can be exceeded due to abrupt and/or excessive fish additions.

If you find yourself asking the question, "Can I add more fish to my tank ?" the answer likely lies within your inquiry and your aquarium probably already in a state of overpopulation, often resulting from inadequate project planning.

In the event that the advice provided in this section is overlooked, you should certainly anticipate encountering a myriad of issues relatively quickly, which could ultimately lead to frustration and an untimely abandonment of this wonderful passion that is the world of aquaristics !

Which fish are right for a small community aquarium of at least 16 - 26 US gal ?

Our list (fish sheet at the end of the book) :

Rasboras

Lambchop Rasbora (*Trigonostigma espei*)
Neon Rasbora (*Microdevario kubotai*)
Dwarf Rasbora (*Boraras maculatus*)
Mosquito Rasbora or Chili Rasboras (*Boraras brigittae*)
Least Rasbora or Exclamation point Rasbora (*Boraras urophthalmoides*)

Tetras

X-ray Tetra or X-ray fish (*Pristella maxillaris*)
Ember Tetra (*Hyphessobrycon amandae*)
Silvertip Tetra (*Hasemania nana*)
Ruby Tetra (*Axelrodia riesei*)

Danios

Spotted Danio (*Danio nigrofasciatus*)
Gold Ring Danio (*Danio tinwini*)
Emerald Dwarf Danio (*Danio erythromicron*)

Corydoras

Pygmy Corydoras (*Corydoras pygmaeus*)
Salt and Pepper Corydoras (*Corydoras habrosus*)
Dwarf Corydoras (*Corydoras hastatus*)

Community aquarium

Poecilias

Common Guppy (*Poecilia reticulata*)
Endler's Guppy (*Poecilia wingei*)
Platy (*Xiphophorus maculatus*)

 Please note that these species are highly prolific and can potentially lead to overpopulation in the tank within a few months.

Other Species

Apistogramma (*Borellii* or *Hongsloi*)
Least Killifish (*Heterandria formosa*)
Honey Gourami (*Trichogaster chuna*)
Peacock Gudgeon (*Tateurndina ocellicauda*)
Hillstream Loach (*Gastromyzon punctulatus*)
Betta Fish (*Betta splendens*) – 1 male or multiple females
Ram Cichlid (*Mikrogeophagus ramirezi*)

Invertebrates

Neocaridina Davidi Shrimp
Japonica or Amano Shrimp (*Caridina multidentata*)

CPO Crayfish (*Cambarellus patzcuarensis*)
Dwarf Crayfish (*Cambarellus diminutus*)

Zebra Apple Snail (*Asolene spixi*)
Diadem Snail (*Clithon diadema*)
Nerite Snail (*Variegata, Natalensis, Turrita, ...*)
Ramshorn Snail

Community aquarium

Co-habitation possible in 16 - 26 US gal

	Rasboras	Tetras	Danios	Corydoras	Poecilias	Betta	Ramirezi	Invertebrates
Rasboras	✓	✗	✗	✓	✗	✓	✓	✓
Tetras	✗	✓	✗	✓	✗	✓	✓	✓
Danios	✗	✗	✓	✓	✗	✗	✓	✗
Corydoras	✓	✓	✓	✓	✓	✓	✓	✓
Poecilias	✗	✗	✗	✓	✓	✗	✓	✓
Betta	✓	✓	✗	✓	✗	✗	✓	✗
Ramirezi	✓	✓	✓	✓	✓	✓	✓	✗
Invertebrates	✓	✓	✗	✓	✓	✗	✗	✓

ACCORDING TO THE FISH

The specific aquarium

A species-specific aquarium is a simpler and more beginner-friendly type of aquarium. Unlike a community aquarium, the specific tank focuses exclusively on one type of fish, which greatly eases the learning curve. Moreover, certain species demand exclusive maintenance in a specific aquarium due to their specific needs, behaviors, or lifestyle. Finally, any tank with a volume less than 16 US gal should typically house only one type of fish (with a few exceptions), making them ideal for species-specific setups.

Population

A pecific aquarium allows for the possibility of keeping any fish species, with the primary and consistent requirement being to adhere to the specific needs of that particular species and not exceeding the aquarium's capacity in terms of the number of fish. Some species are perfectly suited for this type of setup, such as shrimp, crayfish, various killifish, and cichlids. These species can be territorial or even aggressive towards other species, or conversely, they may be vulnerable to predation by other fish. It is advisable to dedicate a separate tank to them to prevent potential conflicts and fully enjoy observing their natural behaviors.

Installation

Once again, there are no specific layout rules for a specific aquarium other than meeting the needs of the chosen fish species to the best extent possible. A beginner's specific aquarium can have a volume smaller than what is recommended for a community aquarium, but it's generally advisable to avoid extremely small nano tanks for your initial experience (see the next page for details). For a beginner, a 13 US gal / 11 UK gal tank with a species of fish that suits this volume (see fish profiles) is a great choice to start with. To make it unique, you can further enhance its aesthetic appeal by exploring biotope or aquascaping-style decorations (see page 95).

ACCORDING TO THE FISH

The nanoaquarium

In recent years, "nano tanks" have become increasingly popular, attracting the interest of beginners in particular. Indeed, on paper, nano aquariums seem to offer many advantages. They come with a lower overall cost, occupy less space, are easier to set up and maintain and often feature stylish designs, such as the absence of visible seams between the panoramic front glass and the side panels. However, it's worth noting that nano tanks also come with some notable disadvantages.

An even smaller world, with a fragile balance

Before delving further into this type of aquarium, we firmly believe that its minimum volume should be at least **5 US gal / 4 UK gal**. Below this volume, in our view, no animal species would be suitable for satisfactory maintenance.

The main drawback of the nano aquarium is, in fact, also its primary characteristic: its small size. Compared to larger tanks, a nano aquarium has significantly less inertia. This means that even minor disruptions can quickly upset its balance and stability. Therefore, you need to be even more vigilant when it comes to maintaining and monitoring your tank to immediately detect any issues that could prove fatal :

- Water temperature can rise rapidly in a small volume during the summer.
- Pollution levels may reach a critical threshold more quickly (due to reduced biological filtration capacity and less water for diluting nitrogenous compounds).
- Algae can proliferate more easily and rapidly, covering a small surface and volume.

In this setup, any mistake, whether made by a beginner or an experienced hobbyist, can have detrimental consequences. That's why nano aquariums are generally not recommended for those new to the hobby.

A limited population

With limited space, the choice of species is also restricted. It's essential to keep in mind that it's not the adult size of the fish that determines its suitability for a small aquarium but rather its behavior and needs. For instance, you should exclude all schooling fish, no matter how small they are, as they are good swimmers and require substantial swimming space (a minimum of 60 cm / 24 inch in length for the smallest). Below is a list of fish and invertebrates that are suitable for a nano aquarium.

The nanoaquarium

What type of fish for a nano aquarium (between 5 and 10 US gal) ?

Our list :

For aquarium volumes between 5 and 8 US gal :

- 1 betta fish (Betta splendens) with long fin types like veiltail, halfmoon, crowntail, etc. Please note that the "plakat" forms (males with short fins) and females are strong swimmers and should be housed in a minimum of 9 – 11 US gal.

or

- 10 Dwarf Shrimp (*Neocaridina davidi* or *Caridina cantonensis*)

+

- Snails (*Neritina, Clithon*)

For aquarium volumes greater than 8 US gal :

- 1 betta fish (Betta splendens)

or

A pair of Killifish (10 US gal / 8 UK gal minimum for a trio of 1 male and 2 females) :
  - Lyretail panchax or Cape Lopez lyretail (*Aphyosemion australe*)
  - Clown Killifish or banded panchax (*Epiplatys annulatus*)
  - Redtail notho (*Nothobranchius guentheri*)

or

- A pair or trio of CPO Crayfish (*Cambarellus patzcuarensis*)

or

- A trio of Dwarf pufferfish (*Carinotetraodon travancoricus*)

or

- 10 Dwarf Shrimp (*Neocaridina davidi* or *Caridina cantonensis*)

+

- Snails (Neritina, Clithon)

ACCORDING TO THE DECOR

The biotope aquarium

The biotope aquarium is a distinctive style of aquarium design with the objective of faithfully replicating the natural ecosystem of a specific region in the world. It should encompass nearly all the elements of that place, including identical water parameters, lighting conditions, aquatic landscapes, as well as the same flora and fauna species. Consequently, there are numerous feasible biotopes to recreate, each one distinct from the others: the Amazonian biotope with its diverse aquatic environments, the Asian biotope with its mountainous swift-flowing rivers, rice paddies, or tranquil streams, the African biotope featuring the rivers and vast lakes like Malawi, Tanganyika, or Victoria, and the Australo-Guinean biotope that encompasses lakes and waterways stretching from Indonesia to Australia. This section serves the sole purpose of conveying the essence of this type of aquarium and is not intended to provide detailed explanations for creating each biotope. We will only delve into two of the most common ones : an example of an Asian biotope and a description of Amazonian biotopes.

The Asian biotope

Creating an Asian biotope in your aquarium is relatively straightforward, given the wide variety of fish and plant species available in the market. However, it's important to note that merely sharing a geographical origin does not guarantee compatibility within the same aquarium. For instance, bettas, gouramis, or colisas are naturally found in calm, shallow waters such as rice paddy ditches and are not suited to coexist with species native to turbulent mountainous rivers, like Tanichthys, Danios, or Gastromyzon. In the latter case, you'll need to ensure there is more substantial water circulation and turbulence in the aquarium.

A potential setup for an Asian biotope aquarium might include :

- A 32 US gal (26 UK gal) tank with a low water outflow (oriented against one of the aquarium walls for instance, to diminish its force).
- A peat bogwood adorned with Java moss and Java fern (*Microsorum pteropus*).
- A selection of plants like Cryptocorynes, Riccia, and Hygrophila.
- A community of 10 Rasboras and a pair of Colisa fish.

The Amazon biotope

The Amazonian biotope, as its name suggests, aims to replicate the rivers and banks of the famous Amazon River, which flows through a significant portion of South America. With a length exceeding 6400 kilometers and covering several million square kilometers, it stands as one of the world's largest rivers. Given its vast expanse, it offers unparalleled biodiversity, characterized by three main types: clearwater, whitewater, and blackwater. These distinctions represent biotopes with diverse physical and chemical parameters and appearances.

The "clearwater" can be found in less turbulent rivers originating from mountainous regions where water erosion on rocks is minimal. Consequently, it contains very few sediments, making it exceptionally soft (with a GH lower than 1) and, in some areas, slightly acidic (with a pH ranging from 4.5 to 7.5). While the waterbed may be quite deep and rocky, with limited aquatic vegetation, the riverbanks are richer in flora, and the roots of neighboring trees provide numerous hiding spots for the fish residing there, such as Corydoras, Apistogramma, Discus, Pterophyllum, and Astronotus.

The "whitewater" is slightly opaque, with an ochre/yellow hue, offering limited visibility (less than 50 centimeters / 20 inch). It fills rivers with occasionally rapid currents, originating from mountains that release a plethora of nutrients and minerals. Nonetheless, the water remains relatively soft and close to neutral (with a pH between 6.2 and 7). These conditions are not conducive to the growth of aquatic plants, which are sparse, but they greatly favor the development of trees and marshland and terrestrial plants, creating a dense forest in the vicinity. A substantial organic mass, composed of fallen wood and leaves, carpets the riverbed.

The "blackwater" is characterized by a dark brown coloration, resulting from the high concentration of humic acids originating from significant organic matter in decomposition (leaves, wood, fruits, etc). Nevertheless, the water is not at all turbid but rather clear, offering decent visibility (between 1 and 2 meters). It is also very soft (with GH almost at 0) and highly acidic (with a pH ranging from 3.5 to 5). Given these parameters, few plants thrive in this environment, and the fish inhabiting it, such as some Discus or certain Hyphessobrycon species, seek refuge in dead wood and the roots of large trees along the waterways.

ACCORDING TO THE DECOR

The aquascaping aquarium

Aquascaping, a specialized field within the realm of aquarium keeping, places a strong emphasis on aesthetics. This pertains not only to the landscape created within the tank but also extends to the design and purification of the overall equipment. This includes features like ultra-clear glass tank walls, transparent seals, glass or stainless steel piping fittings, mandatory CO2 systems, and high-performance, stylish LED lighting fixtures. Aquascaping requires a relatively substantial level of knowledge and experience in the realm of aquarium maintenance, often accompanied by a budget larger than what's typical for a conventional aquarium. Much like biotope aquariums, there are various styles of aquascaping to explore.

The Nature Aquarium (NA style)

Invented and popularized by the renowned Japanese photographer and aquarist Takashi Amano, the Nature Aquarium aims to recreate the most natural and wild landscapes possible by skillfully, thoughtfully, and harmoniously combining rocks, roots, and plants. In contrast to the biotope aquarium, the focus here lies solely on the aesthetic arrangement of the scenery, without concerning itself with adhering to the geographical origin of the elements or fish.

The Dutch aquarium

Often considered the precursor of modern aquascaping, the Dutch aquarium distinguishes itself through the complete absence of hardscape elements such as rocks and roots. The decor is solely composed of a rich and diverse array of plants, delicately coordinated through the interplay of color, shape, and leaf size. This type of aquarium owes its name to the country of its origin, where it emerged in the 1950s. These were the first aquariums in the field of aquaristics to prioritize the emphasis on plants and their aesthetic presentation.

The aquascaping aquarium

The Iwagumi

Increasingly popular, the Iwagumi style originates from Japan and draws inspiration from the zen art of traditional stone gardens. The aquarium is exclusively composed of rocks, often using Seiryu stone, along with typically low-lying or carpeting plants. To adhere to the authentic Iwagumi principles, there are strict rules governing the sizes and placement of various stones, often following the "rule of thirds" or the "Golden ratio." This meticulous arrangement is intended to ensure that the stones dominate the entire landscape. Plants, in this style, serve the sole purpose of gracefully adorning the spaces and conveying the effect of a serene, verdant plain. The most commonly used plants for this purpose include *Glossostigma elatinoides*, *Hemianthus callitrichoides cuba*, and *Eleocharis tenellus*.

Less traditional styles of Iwagumi

Treescape and Forestscape

A distinct form of aquascaping, the aim here is to recreate the illusion of a single (Treescape) or multiple (Forestscape) submerged trees at the bottom of the aquarium. To achieve this effect, a carefully selected (or adapted) piece of driftwood is often used to form the tree trunk and branches, adorned with one or several clumps of aquatic mosses to mimic the foliage. The most commonly depicted trees in this style are the renowned bonsai trees, for which corresponding root shapes can be readily purchased in the market. However, numerous other tree forms can also be explored.

Different styles of trees and forests (more or less happy !)

The aquascaping aquarium

Mountainscape

Following a similar principle to the Forestscape, the objective here is to create the illusion of underwater cliffs or canyons. To achieve this effect, a substantial amount of rocks of the same type but varying in size is required to replicate a scaled-down mountainous terrain. A more or less pronounced planting (depending on the desired landscape) is used to adorn and introduce a touch of green to this terrestrial setting.

Different Mountainscape styles

Information sheets

The collection of data sheets (for fish and plants) in this section aims to provide you with the most pertinent and essential information for each species presented. All the recommendations and guidelines provided in these sheets are considered "ideal" and are based on either scientific data from the species' natural habitat or on accumulated maintenance experiences to achieve these results. However, it is possible that not all the information provided may be suitable or applicable in certain specific cases and for certain animals.

To minimize the risk of acclimation and adaptation failures for your animals in your aquarium, always inquire about the origin of your fish, the type of maintenance they received previously, and any potential specific needs they may have. This way, you can cross-reference this information with the data in the sheets and make the necessary adjustments to your aquarium to best accommodate your future inhabitants.

Legende :

| Fish sheets | Plants sheets | Diseases sheets |

♥ : Lifespan

★★★★ : Maintenance Difficulty (1 star easy, 5 stars difficult)

💡💡💡 : Light Requirement (1 light low requirement, 3 lights high requirement)

CO_2 : CO_2 Injection

 : Nutrient supplementation (nutrient-rich substrate, sticks, liquid fertilizers, etc)

FISH SHEETS – NANOAQUARIUM OF AT LEAST 5 GAL

Betta fish (*Betta Splendens*)

: 2 to 4 years

Origin

Needs
A minimum of 5 US gal (4,5 UK gal) aquarium, it adapts to most water parameters but prefers rather soft water (between 5 and 10°GH) and slightly acidic water (pH between 6.5 and 7.5). A temperature between 75 and 82°F.

Behavior
Territorial, several males should not be kept together. Cohabitation of females and other species (except "veiled" fish such as guppy, molly, gouramis, colisas...) is perfectly possible. Beware, however, of fish likely to attack its fins (danios, bearded fish, etc).

Description
Between 5 and 8 cm (2 and 3 inch), males are larger and more colorful than females with generally longer fins (except for plakat forms, as shown here).

Shrimp (*Neocaridina Davidi*)

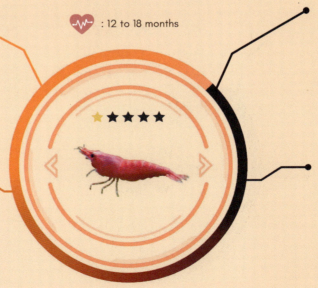

: 12 to 18 months

Origin

Needs
A planted aquarium of at least 5 US gal (4,5 UK gal) is recommended for this species. It can adapt to various water parameters but thrives in slightly soft and mildly acidic water. Maintain a temperature range between 40 and 82°F.

Behavior
A gregarious species, it should be kept in a group of at least 5 individuals, which will reproduce quickly under suitable maintenance conditions. Peaceful in nature, it should not be housed with carnivores that may mistake it for prey.

Description
A small species averaging 2 cm (0,8 inch) in size, which has become the most popular shrimp in the realm of aquarium keeping, primarily due to its wide range of colors (red, orange, yellow, blue, brown, green, etc.) and ease of maintenance.

FISH SHEETS - NANOAQUARIUM OF AT LEAST **8 GAL**

Cape Lopez Lyretail
(Aphyosemion australe)

♥ : 2 years

Origin

Needs
A minimum of a 8 US gal (6 UK gal) aquarium with dense vegetation and subdued lighting (using floating plants) is recommended for this species. The water should be maintained at a moderate temperature between 68 and 75°F, slightly acidic (pH 6 to 7) and soft (5 to 10°GH).

Behavior
A relatively peaceful fish that is best kept in a species-specific aquarium, either as a couple or a trio (1 male for every 2 females). Males may exhibit some aggression towards females, so it's advisable to provide a tank with ample plants and hiding spots. Please note that this species is an excellent jumper, so ensure that the aquarium is fully covered.

Description
The most renowned species within the killifish family, it stands out due to its coloring, ranging from yellow-orange to red, with red spots on its body and head. The male is larger than the female (6 cm / 2,3 inch compared to 5 cm / 2 inch) and much more vibrantly colored.

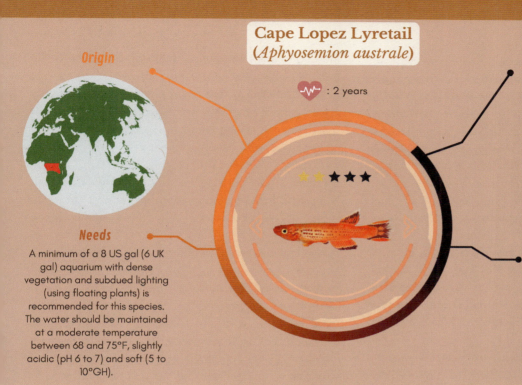

Clown Killifish
(Pseudepiplatys annulatus)

♥ : 3 years

Origin

Needs
A minimum of a 8 US gal (6 UK gal) aquarium with dense vegetation and subdued lighting (using of floating plants) is recommended for this species. The water should be maintained at a moderate temperature between 68 and 75°F, slightly acidic (pH 5.5 to 6.8) and soft (3 to 8°GH).

Behavior
A relatively peaceful fish that is best kept in a species-specific aquarium, either as a couple or a trio (1 male for every 2 females). Males may exhibit some aggression towards females, so it's advisable to provide a tank with ample plants and hiding spots. Please note that this species is an excellent jumper, so ensure that the aquarium is fully covered.

Description
At just under 3cm (1,2 inch) when fully grown, this species is characterized by a body striped vertically in yellow and black, with electric blue eyes and tail tips. The females are paler with colorless fins.

FISH SHEETS - NANOAQUARIUM OF AT LEAST 8 GAL

Redtail Notho
(*Nothonbranchius guentheri*)

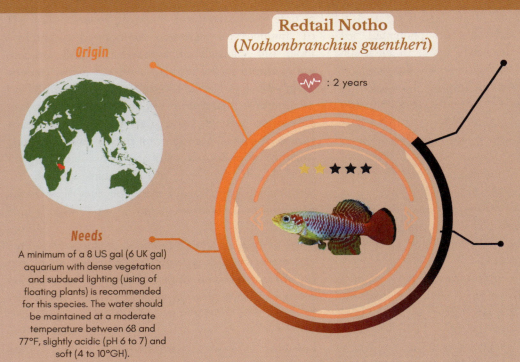

♥ : 2 years

Origin

Needs

A minimum of a 8 US gal (6 UK gal) aquarium with dense vegetation and subdued lighting (using of floating plants) is recommended for this species. The water should be maintained at a moderate temperature between 68 and 77°F, slightly acidic (pH 6 to 7) and soft (4 to 10°GH).

Behavior

Like other killifish, it is relatively peaceful but it is best to keep it in a species-specific aquarium, either as a couple or a trio (1 male for every 2 females). Males may exhibit some signs of aggression towards females, so it's advisable to provide a tank with plenty of plants and hiding spots. Please note that this species is an excellent jumper, so ensure that the aquarium is fully covered.

Description

One of the most colorful killifish species, the males are tricolored, featuring a gradient of colors ranging from yellow to red, with shades of blue-green. The females, on the other hand, are yellow with blue highlights. This killifish typically measures around 4 to 5 cm (1,5 to 2 inch) on average.

Dwarf Pufferfish
(*Carinotetraodon travancoricus*)

♥ : 5 years

Origin

Needs

A planted aquarium with a minimum of 8 US gal (6 UK gal) is recommended. These fish are heavy waste producers, necessitating an appropriate filtration system with a flow rate of at least 4 times the volume of the tank. The water should be maintained at a temperature between 75 and 79°F, slightly alkaline (pH 7 to 8) and moderately hard (10 to 20°GH).

Behavior

This species is shy and extremely timid, so providing numerous hiding places is essential to reassure them. Being carnivorous, they prey on shrimp and snails, and they may also nip at the fins of other fish. Therefore, it's advisable to keep them in a species-specific aquarium with a minimum of two or three individuals.

Description

The Dwarf Puffer, one of the smallest pufferfish in the world, has an average adult size of 3 cm (1,2 inch). Its body is two-toned, white on the belly and golden-yellow on the upper part, adorned with black marbled patterns.

FISH SHEETS - NANOAQUARIUM OF AT LEAST 8 GAL

CPO Crayfish
(*Cambarellus patzcuarensis*)

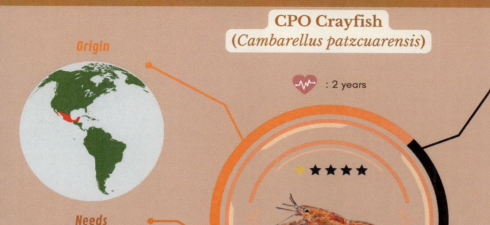

: 2 years

Origin

Needs
A minimum of a 8 US gal (6 UK gal) planted aquarium with two hiding spots per crayfish is recommended. These crayfish are relatively tolerant due to their geographical origin. Therefore, the water conditions can be on the harder side (between 10 and 20°GH), slightly alkaline (pH between 7 and 8.5), and maintained at a temperature between 59 and 77 °F.

Behavior
This species lives in extended groups and should be maintained in at least 2 or even 3 individuals. They are generally peaceful, but territorial and aggressive behaviors can surface if there is insufficient space or food, and they may even exhibit cannibalism. Coexisting with small fish is possible, but it's best to avoid bottom-dwelling species like Corydoras.

Description
Dwarf crayfish typically reach an average size of 3 cm (1,2 inch) or 4 cm (1,6 inch) for females. They are usually orange in color (brown in the wild) and feature white horizontal stripes along their bodies.

Spotted Nerite
Vittina natalensis

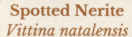

: 1 years

Origin

Needs
Suitable for aquariums of all sizes, it can thrive in a wide range of mineralized water (GH > 4°) with a pH level between 6 and 8 and at a temperature between 72° and 81 °F.

Behavior
A voracious algae eater, it can prove to be more effective in this task than shrimp (like Amano shrimp) or fish (such as Otocinclus). You may observe it roaming on any surface within the aquarium, and it may even venture out if there is no lid!

Description
With an average size of 2 to 3 cm (0,8 to 1,2 inch), Spotted Nerite encompass various species with diverse patterns and colors on their shells. The brilliance of their shells is directly influenced by the mineral content of the water.

FISH SHEETS - 10 TO 30 GAL

Pygmy Corydoras
(*Corydoras Pygmaeus*)

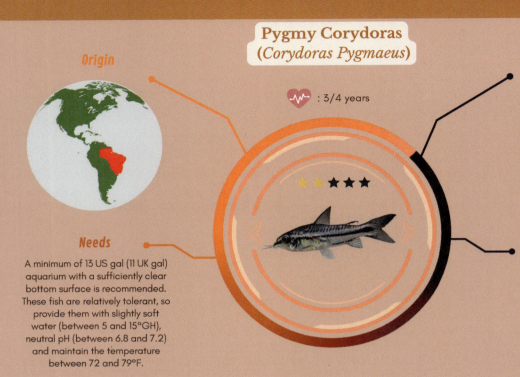

: 3/4 years

Origin

Needs

A minimum of 13 US gal (11 UK gal) aquarium with a sufficiently clear bottom surface is recommended. These fish are relatively tolerant, so provide them with slightly soft water (between 5 and 15°GH), neutral pH (between 6.8 and 7.2) and maintain the temperature between 72 and 79°F.

Behavior

A calm and gregarious fish that thrives in small groups of at least 10 individuals. It mainly resides at the bottom of the aquarium and tends to hide in the presence of larger fish. It should have ample space on the substrate for digging. Be cautious with the choice of substrate, which should not be abrasive to its barbels (e.g., quartz).

Description

With an average size of 3,5 cm (1,4 inch), like all Corydoras, it has barbels for digging in the substrate and bony plates in place of scales. It is recognizable by the black stripe running along the entire length of its body and its silvery back.

Salt and pepper Catfish
(*Corydoras Habrosus*)

: 5 years

Origin

Needs

A minimum of 13 US gal (11 UK gal) aquarium with a sufficiently clear bottom surface is recommended. These fish are somewhat sensitive, so provide them with relatively soft water (5 to 12°GH), slightly acidic (pH 6.2 to 7) and maintain the temperature between 72 and 82°F.

Behavior

A peaceful fish that needs to live in a group of at least 10 individuals to feel secure. It primarily resides at the bottom of the aquarium but can swim in open water. Quite lively and curious, it enjoys moving between plants but should have enough space on the substrate for digging. Be cautious with the choice of substrate, as it should not be abrasive to the barbels of these fish (e.g., quartz).

Description

One of the smallest corydoras, with an average adult size of 3 cm (1,2 inch), characterized by its translucent white body and black spots, earning it the nickname "salt and pepper."

FISH SHEETS - 10 TO 30 GAL

Emerald Dwarf Danio
(Danio erythromicron)

: 3 years

Origin

Needs
A planted aquarium with a minimum capacity of 20 US gal (16 UK gal) is recommended, featuring aquatic mosses, which are particularly well-regarded. Given its mountainous origin, this species exhibits a considerable degree of tolerance. The water conditions should align with moderately to high hardness (15 to 20°GH), a slightly alkaline nature (pH 7 to 8) and a temperature between 68 and 73°F.

Behavior
A rather timid and social species, it thrives best when kept in a collective of 15 to 20 individuals to foster a sense of security. Its predominant swimming behavior occurs near the water's surface and at a mid-level within the aquarium, displaying an energetic demeanor. To ensure its well-being, it is advisable to house it alongside fish of similar temperament and ideally matching in size for a reassuring environment.

Description
A diminutive fish, not surpassing 3 cm (1,2 inch) in adulthood. It boasts a splendid attire adorned with striped patterns of vibrant blue hues and fins tinted in a captivating shade of orange.

Spotted Danio or Dwarf Danio
(Danio Nigrofasciatus)

: 3/4 years

Origin

Needs
A planted aquarium with a minimum capacity of 15 US gal (13 UK gal) is recommended. This species demonstrates adaptability to water conditions ranging from neutral to slightly acidic (pH 6 to 7.5), a preference for soft water (2 to 10°GH) and a temperature range of 64 to 77°F.

Behavior
A social species by nature, it thrives best when kept in a group of at least 8 individuals to mitigate stress. Possessing a notably tranquil disposition, it is advisable to house it alongside fish of similar temperament and ideally matching in size. Please be aware that they are proficient jumpers, so ensure proper coverage for their aquarium.

Description
Small fish with an average size of 4 cm (1,5 inch), it is distinguishable by its golden hue, bluish-black spots, and a distinctive longitudinal stripe stretching from its gills to its tail.

FISH SHEETS - 10 TO 30 GAL

Common guppy
(*Poecilia Reticulata*)

♥ : 2/3 years

Origin

Needs

A minimum of 15 US gal (13 UK gal) aquarium is recommended to accommodate the anticipated frequent reproductions. The guppy demonstrates adaptability to a wide range of water conditions, with a pH tolerance between 5.5 and 8, a GH ranging from 5° to 18° and a temperature between 59 and 83 °F.

Behavior

An energetic species, remarkably easy to maintain and integrate into a community. It predominantly swims near the water's surface. Known for its prolific breeding, it is recommended to keep these fish with a minimum ratio of 1 male to 3 females, or exclusively among males. The males can be quite assertive with the females, potentially leading to exhaustion and even mortality if the male-to-female ratio is not carefully observed.

Description

One of the most renowned exotic fish species, distinguished by the larger size of the females (5 cm / 2 inch compared to 3 cm / 1,2 inch for males) and their comparatively subdued coloration. The males, on the other hand, showcase elongated flowing fins and display a vibrant array of colors.

Common platy
(*Xiphophorus Maculatus*)

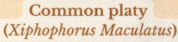

♥ : 3 years

Origin

Needs

A well-planted aquarium with a minimum capacity of 21 US gal (17 UK gal) is recommended. These fish thrive in slightly basic water conditions, with a pH ranging from 7 to 8, GH between 10 and 25° and a maintained temperature of 72 to 77°F.

Behavior

Similar to the guppy, the platy is highly adaptable and tends to swim near the water's surface or mid-level. Even more prolific, a pair (platys form monogamous partnerships) can yield a substantial offspring within a few months. To prevent the potential exhaustion of the female, it is advisable to ensure a well-planted aquarium, providing ample hiding spaces for her refuge.

Description

The females surpass the males in size (up to 7 cm / 3 inch compared to 4 cm / 1,5 inch for males). Platys exhibit a broad spectrum of colors, but their fundamental hue is orange/red, often accompanied by varying degrees of black on their fins.

FISH SHEETS - 10 TO 30 GAL

Apistogramma Hongsloi

❤ : 5 years

Origin

Needs
A well-planted aquarium with a minimum capacity of 21 US gal (17 UK gal) is recommended. This fish, known for its resilience, thrives in water conditions that are notably soft (GH 1 to 6°), slightly acidic (pH 6.5 to 7.2) and kept warm (between 73 and 79°F).

Behavior
The Apistogramma Hongsloi naturally dwells in pairs, typically near the bottom of the aquarium. Despite its generally calm and even shy temperament, signs of aggression may manifest in confined spaces (less than 25 gallon), especially when sharing the same swimming zone with other species exhibiting similar behavior.

Description
Belonging to the family of Amazonian dwarf cichlids, it attains a size ranging from 5 to 7 cm (2 to 3 inch). Various color varieties exist, with the wild form distinguished by a silvery body transitioning to a rosy hue at the extremities, complemented by an orangish-yellow head.

Honey Gourami
(Trichogaster Chuna)

❤ : 3 years

Origin

Needs
A heavily planted aquarium with a minimum capacity of 16 US gal (14 UK gal) is recommended. This species is adaptable to a broad range of water parameters but thrives best in relatively soft water (between 3 and 12 °GH), slightly acidic conditions (pH 6.5 to 7), and a temperature range of 72°C to 82°F.

Behavior
Quiet yet territorial, particularly during the breeding season. Best kept in pairs or preferably in a trio with one male for every two females. Given their somewhat slow pace, careful attention is needed to ensure they obtain an ample quantity of food without being outpaced by more active species that might seize their sustenance.

Description
Despite being small for a gourami at 5 cm (2 inch), it belongs to the same family as the betta fish. Upon reaching adulthood, the male exhibits a distinctive yellow-orange hue, earning it the moniker "honey gourami." Conversely the female is more subdued, displaying a gray-beige color with hints of a bluish sheen.

FISH SHEETS - 10 TO 30 GAL

Lambchop Rasbora (*Trigonostigma Espei*)

♥ : 2 years

Origin

Needs
A minimum of 15 US gal (13 UK gal) aquarium with a frontage of at least 60 cm (24 inch) in length is recommended. Enrich the habitat with substantial vegetation and maintain the water conditions to be soft (1 to 10°GH), slightly acidic (pH 5.5 to 6.5), and kept within the temperature range of 73 to 81°F.

Behavior
Being a schooling fish, it is imperative to maintain it in a group of at least 8 to 10 individuals. With a peaceful temperament, it can coexist harmoniously with any other fish species of similar disposition and size. It tends to become more inconspicuous in the presence of larger fish. Additionally, it is advisable to avoid pairing it with fish that occupy the same swimming zone, particularly those in the upper or middle regions of the aquarium.

Description
Frequently mistaken for the Harlequin Rasbora (*Trigonostigma heteromorpha*), this species distinguishes itself by a slender, hatchet-shaped black mark on its body. Additionally, it is smaller in size, averaging around 3 cm (1 inch).

Green neon Rasbora (*Microdevario Kubotai*)

♥ : 3/4 years

Origin

Needs
Despite its small size, it requires a minimum of 15 US gal (13 UK gal) aquarium with a frontage of at least 60 cm (24 inch). Opt for moderately dense vegetation and maintain the water conditions to be relatively soft (3 to 10°GH), slightly acidic (pH 6 to 7) and kept within the temperature range of 72 to 79°F.

Behavior
A schooling fish, it is crucial for its well-being to live in a group of at least 12 individuals to feel secure. Otherwise, it may become timid and stressed, displaying faded colors. Highly lively and active, it requires a spacious swimming area, free from any obstructing elements such as decorations or plants. Despite its lively nature, it maintains a peaceful demeanor and can coexist harmoniously with other species of similar temperament.

Description
One of the smallest aquarium fish, measuring between 1 and 2 cm (0,4 to 0,8 inch), it derives its name from its emerald-green coloration. Male and female specimens closely resemble each other but the male tends to be slightly more vibrant in color and smaller in size.

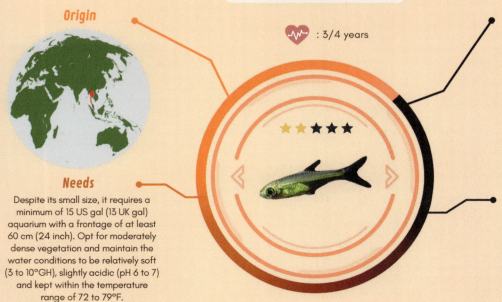

FISH SHEETS - 10 TO 30 GAL

Dwarf Rasbora
(*Boraras Maculatus*)

♥ : 3 years

Origin

Needs

A minimum of 15 US gal (13 UK gal) aquarium with a frontage of at least 60 cm (24 inch) is recommended. Cultivate abundant vegetation and maintain the water conditions to be relatively soft (3 to 10°GH), slightly acidic (pH 5 to 6.5) and kept within the temperature range of 73 to 81 °F.

Behavior

A schooling fish, it is essential to maintain it in a group of at least 10 individuals. Being lively and adept swimmers, it requires an aquarium with sufficient length to navigate the midsection comfortably. With a peaceful temperament, it can harmoniously coexist with other fish species of similar disposition and size. It tends to adopt a more inconspicuous behavior in the presence of larger fish.

Description

Small fish averaging 2 cm (0,8 inch) in length, it possesses an slender body and showcases a predominantly orange hue, marked by distinctive black spots: one along the midsection of the body, another at the base of the anal fin, and a third at the base of the caudal fin.

Mosquito Rasbora
(*Boraras Brigittae*)

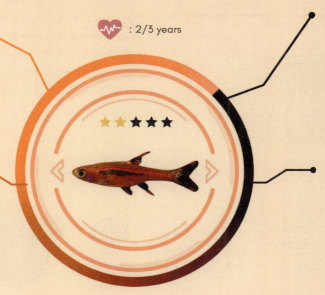

♥ : 2/3 years

Origin

Needs

A minimum of 15 US gal (13 UK gal) aquarium with a frontage measuring at least 60 cm (24 inch) is recommended. Cultivate lush vegetation and maintain the water conditions to be relatively soft (1 to 8°GH), slightly acidic (pH 5 to 6.5) and kept a temperature between 73 and 81 °F.

Behavior

A schooling fish, it is imperative to maintain it in a group of at least 10 to 12 individuals. With a peaceful temperament, it can peacefully coexist with other fish species of similar disposition and size. It tends to adopt a more inconspicuous behavior in the presence of larger fish. Caution is advised, as it is an adept jumper.

Description

Measuring between 2 to 3 cm (0,8 to 1,2 inch) and exhibiting an oval shape, this fish boasts a distinctive red-orange coloration. It is characterized by a silver-black midline stripe and a small spot at the base of the caudal fin. The male, smaller in size, displays more vibrant colors.

FISH SHEETS - 10 TO 30 GAL

Ember Tetra
(*Hyphessobrycon Amandae*)

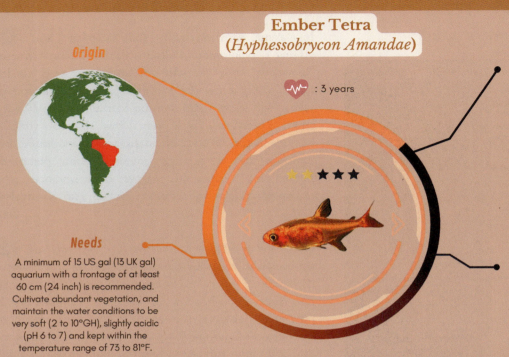

Origin

♥ : 3 years

Needs

A minimum of 15 US gal (13 UK gal) aquarium with a frontage of at least 60 cm (24 inch) is recommended. Cultivate abundant vegetation, and maintain the water conditions to be very soft (2 to 10°GH), slightly acidic (pH 6 to 7) and kept within the temperature range of 73 to 81°F.

Behavior

A schooling fish, it is imperative to maintain it in a group of at least 10 to 12 individuals. Highly active and a proficient swimmer, it requires an aquarium with sufficient length to navigate the midsection comfortably. With a peaceful temperament, it can harmoniously coexist with other fish species of similar disposition and size. It tends to adopt a more inconspicuous behavior in the presence of larger fish.

Description

A small fish, averaging around 2 cm (0,8 inch) in length, with a slender body. It is unicolored, typically exhibiting a shade of orange. The male is generally smaller but more vibrant in color compared to the female.

Silvertip Tetra
(*Hasemania Nana*)

Origin

♥ : 3 years

Needs

A minimum of 20 US gal (16 UK gal) aquarium (with a frontage of at least 80 cm or 30 inch) is recommended, densely planted. Fairly robust, the optimal water parameters for its upkeep include a neutral pH between 6.8 and 7.2, a low GH between 3° and 10° and a temperature between 72 and 79°F.

Behavior

A quiet specie that interacts minimally with other species. As a schooling fish, it thrives best when kept in groups of at least 10 to 15 individuals. Energetic and proficient in swimming, it predominantly occupies the midsection of the aquarium. It is advisable to avoid cohabitation with species sharing the same swimming space and/or larger counterparts.

Description

A small fish, averaging 3 cm (1,2 inch) in length with a slender body. It earns its name from the golden-orange hue of its attire. The females are more substantial than the males, reaching up to 5cm (2 inch) with a more rounded abdomen.

FISH SHEETS - 10 TO 30 GAL

Ram Cichlid
(*Mikrogeophagus Ramirezi*)

Origin

♥ : 4 years

Behavior

A pacific and shy species, it is advisable to keep the Ramirezi in pairs and alongside other equally peaceful species. The presence of hiding spots will provide reassurance. In a community aquarium, it is unlikely to successfully rear fry to adulthood. Avoid mixing different subspecies of Ramirezi to mitigate the risks of hybridization.

Needs

A minimum of 20 US gal (16 UK gal) aquarium, richly planted, is essential for this somewhat delicate fish. Strict adherence to its requirements is crucial : very soft water (GH between 2° and 6°), slightly acidic (pH between 5 and 6.5) and warm (between 75 and 82°F).

Description

Measuring between 3 and 5 cm (1 to 2 inch), this fish displays a bluish hue with orange/yellow tones towards the head. Males are slightly larger than females, and the latter feature a pinkish spot on their ventral area.

Japanese or Amano shrimp
(*Caridina Multidentata*)

Origin

♥ : 2 years

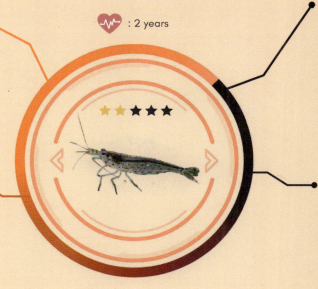

Behavior

A gregarious species, the Japonica shrimp thrives best when kept in a group of at least 5 individuals, allowing you to observe their curious wandering behavior in the aquarium. While generally peaceful, they may occasionally nip at the fins of long-finned fish. It is advisable to avoid cohabitation with significantly larger fish that might mistake them for prey.

Needs

A minimum of 16 US gal (13 UK gal) aquarium, well-planted, is recommended. This species is quite hardy and adapts well to a broad range of parameters, with optimal conditions including a pH 6.5 to 7.5, a GH between 8 and 15° and a temperature between 60 and 82°F.

Description

The first shrimp introduced to the aquarium hobby by the renowned aquascaper Takashi Amano, from whom it derives its name, the Japonica is a relatively large shrimp measuring 4/5 cm (1,5/2 inch), exhibiting a translucent beige-brown coloration.

FISH SHEETS - < 30 GAL

Bushynose (*Ancistrus sp.*)

♥ : 10 years

Origin
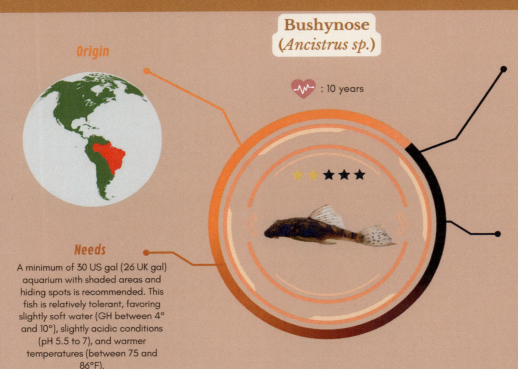

Needs
A minimum of 30 US gal (26 UK gal) aquarium with shaded areas and hiding spots is recommended. This fish is relatively tolerant, favoring slightly soft water (GH between 4° and 10°), slightly acidic conditions (pH 5.5 to 7), and warmer temperatures (between 75 and 86°F).

Behavior
A solitary bottom-dwelling species, it can be kept alone, in pairs, or with two or three females. The male may exhibit signs of aggression and territorial behavior towards other males of its species or other territorial bottom-dwelling species.

Description
Averaging 10 to 13 cm (4 to 5 inch) in size and belonging to the catfish family, it is often incorrectly regarded as the "glass cleaner" fish. Typically brown with white spots, the male can be distinguished from the female by its prominent growths on the snout.

Tiger barb (*Puntigrus tetrazona*)

♥ : 5 years

Origin

Needs
A minimum of 40 US gal (32 UK gal) aquarium, densely planted, is recommended. This fish thrives in slightly acidic water (pH 6 to 6.5), soft water (GH between 1° and 8°), and a temperature range of 77 to 84°F. The presence of "blackwater," colored by tannins, provides a comforting environment.

Behavior
A highly energetic and lively schooling species, it is advisable to maintain it in a group of at least 8 individuals, preferably in a dedicated aquarium. While cohabitation with certain species is possible in a community setup, careful selection of the surrounding population is essential, avoiding fish with overly long fins (as it tends to nip at them).

Description
Bicolored with a predominantly golden body adorned with vertical black stripes. This fish averages between 5 and 7 cm (2 to 2,7 inch) in length.

FISH SHEETS - < 30 GAL

Neon Tetra
(*Paracheirodon innesi*)

♥ : 6 / 7 years

Origin

Needs
A minimum of 30 US gal (25 UK gal) aquarium with subdued lighting (floating plants) and a frontage length of 120 cm (40 inch) is recommended. This somewhat sensitive fish requires strict adherence to its needs : very soft water (GH between 2° and 8°), slightly acidic conditions (ph 5 to 6.5) and warm temperatures (between 75 and 82°F).

Behavior
A gregarious and timid species, it is essential to maintain this fish in a school of at least 12 individuals, preferably in a dedicated aquarium. Being lively and skilled swimmers, providing ample swimming space in the midsection of the tank is crucial for their well-being. The school disperses only when individuals feel secure and promptly regroups at the slightest sign of alert.

Description
Averaging 4 cm (1,5 inch) in size, this fish is characterized by its fluorescent blue and red stripes, from which it derives its name. There is no sexual dimorphism, except for a slightly more rounded belly in females during the breeding period.

Dwarf Gourami
(*Trichogaster lalius*)

♥ : 3 / 4 years

Origin

Needs
A minimum of 25 US gal (20 UK gal) aquarium, well-planted with subdued lighting, is recommended. This relatively sensitive fish requires strict adherence to its needs : soft water (GH between 5° and 12°), slightly acidic conditions (pH 6 to 7.2) and warm temperatures (between 73 and 82°F).

Behavior
A calm yet rather territorial species, especially during the breeding season and interactions with other individuals of its kind. It is best kept either as a pair or alone. Given its relatively slow nature, careful monitoring is necessary to ensure it consumes an adequate amount of food without being outcompeted by more active species in a community aquarium.

Description
Of modest size for a gourami (7 cm / 2,7 inch), it belongs to the same family as the betta. Its natural coloration consists of alternating fine red/orange and blue stripes, but today, there are numerous color variations available.

FISH SHEETS - < 75 GAL

Bluegray Mbuna
(*Pseudotropheus johannii*)

❤️ : 8 years

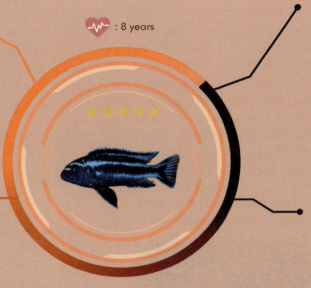

Origin

Needs
A minimum of 75 US gal (60 UK gal) aquarium is required, featuring a setup primarily composed of rocks and crushed shells for the substrate. This species thrives in alkaline water (pH 7.5 to 8.5), relatively hard water (between 10° and 20°GH) and a temperature range of 73 to 82°F.

Behavior
A fish that lives in pairs or small groups consisting of one male and several females, it tends to stay close to the bottom and may engage in digging behavior. Highly territorial, it is advisable to avoid cohabitation with other species that share territorial tendencies and to refrain from keeping multiple males together unless the aquarium size is substantial (130 US gal or 110 UK gal).

Description
Measuring between 3 and 4 inch, this African cichlid is bicolor, with its body adorned with horizontal stripes in black, blue, or yellow. The male can be distinguished from the female by its larger size.

Angelfish
(*Pterophyllum scalare*)

❤️ : 8 / 9 years

Origin

Needs
A minimum of 100 US gal (90 UK gal) aquarium, well-planted with subdued lighting, is recommended. This relatively tolerant fish prefers soft water (GH between 5° and 10°), slightly acidic conditions (pH 6 to 7.2), and a temperature range of 73 to 79°F.

Behavior
A gregarious species, it lives in a hierarchically structured group of at least 8 individuals, predominantly near the water surface. Fairly peaceful, it may exhibit signs of aggression in various contexts : during hunting if there are smaller fish species present, during the breeding season or when interacting with territorial species.

Description
With a potential size ranging from 15 and 20 cm (6 to 8 inch), this species is characterized by its triangular silhouette, formed by the length of its anal and dorsal spiny rays. The base color of the body is gray with four dark vertical bands.

FISH SHEETS - < 75 GAL

Discus
(*Symphysodon aequifasciatus*)

: 5 / 6 years

Origin

Needs
A minimum of 100 US gal (90 UK gal) aquarium with a few plants and roots is necessary. Given its high sensitivity, it is crucial to strictly adhere to suitable parameters, including soft water (GH between 2° and 8°), slightly acidic conditions (pH 5.5 to 6.5) and a temperature range of 79 to 86°F. The water should take on an amber hue due to the release of tannins from the roots.

Behavior
A species exhibiting behavioral fluctuations depending on the periods. Normally gregarious and peaceful, it turns territorial and potentially aggressive during the breeding season. Therefore, it is crucial to provide a sufficient volume for a group of 5 individuals.

Description
Iconic with its compressed circular body, this species is adorned with patterns that can vary based on its origin and can be colored in various shades of blue, brown, red, orange, green, etc. It typically measures between 15 and 20 cm (6 to 8 inch).

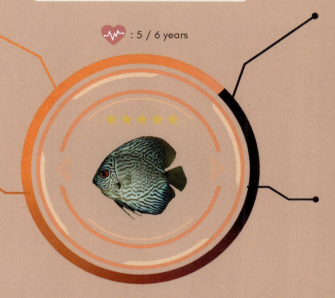

Oscar
(*Astronotus ocellatus*)

: 10 years

Origin

Needs
A minimum of 160 US gal (130 UK gal) aquarium is required for a pair, featuring some plants and roots. This relatively tolerant fish prefers soft water (GH between 5° and 15°), slightly acidic conditions (pH 6 to 6.8) and a temperature range of 72 to 84°F.

Behavior
This species lives in pairs or small groups in the midsection of the aquarium. While generally calm, it can be territorial and may show signs of aggression towards species with similar behavior. Intense interactions can also occur between individuals of the same species, especially in insufficiently sized environments.

Description
A large-sized fish that can reach up to 40 cm (16 inch) in adulthood. Bicolored, it typically has a dark brown/black body adorned with irregular orange spots.

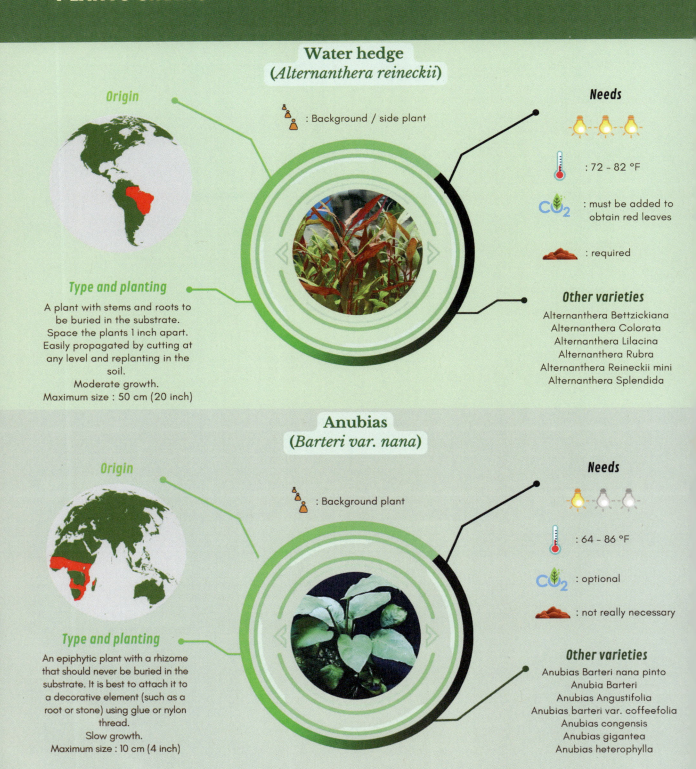

PLANTS SHEETS

Aponogeton (Longiplumulosus)

: Background plant

Origin

Type and planting
A bulb plant to be buried only halfway into the soil. Acclimate it to the new aquarium before planting. Relatively fast growth.
Maximum size : 60 cm (24 inch)

Needs

 : 72 - 79 °F

 : optional

 : optional

Other varieties
Aponogeton Capuronii
Aponogeton Crispus
Aponogeton Crispus Red
Aponogeton Madagascariensis
Aponogeton Ulvaceus

Water hyssop (*Bacopa monnieri*)

: Background plant

Origin

Type and planting
A stem plant with roots to be buried in the substrate. Propagate through cuttings by trimming the stem and replanting it in the soil. Relatively slow growth.
Maximum size : 50 cm (20 inch)

Needs

 : 64 - 82 °F

: optional

: necessary

Other varieties
Bacopa Australis
Bacopa Caroliniana
Bacopa Crenata
Bacopa Lanigera
Bacopa Myriophylloides
Bacopa Rotundifolia

PLANTS SHEETS

African water Fern
(*Bolbitis heudelotii*)

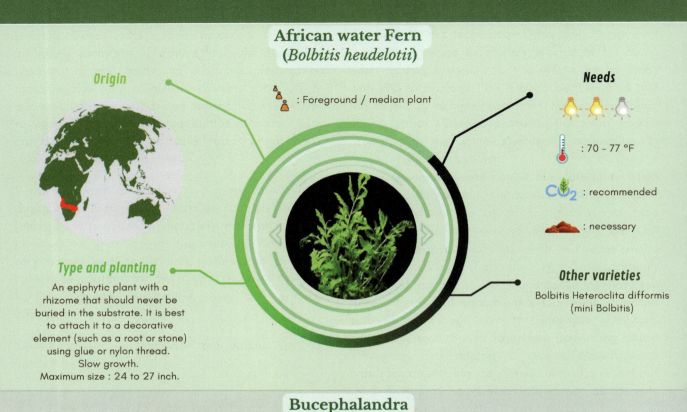

: Foreground / median plant

Origin

Type and planting
An epiphytic plant with a rhizome that should never be buried in the substrate. It is best to attach it to a decorative element (such as a root or stone) using glue or nylon thread. Slow growth.
Maximum size : 24 to 27 inch.

Needs

: 70 – 77 °F

CO_2 : recommended

: necessary

Other varieties
Bolbitis Heteroclita difformis (mini Bolbitis)

Bucephalandra
(Wavy green)

: Foreground plant

Origin

Type and planting
An epiphytic plant with a rhizome that should never be buried in the substrate. It is best to attach it to a decorative element (such as a root or stone) using glue or nylon thread. Slow growth.
Maximum size : 12 cm (5 inch)

Needs

: 68 – 79 °F

CO_2 : optional

: not really necessary

Other varieties
Bucephalandra Alamanda
Bucephalandra Antyovani
Bucephalandra Browni Jade
Bucephalandra Velvet
Bucephalandra Kapuas Hulu
Bucephalandra Lagoon
Bucephalandra Lalina

PLANTS SHEETS

Cabomba (Aquatica)

 : Background plant

Origin

Type and planting
A stem plant with roots to be buried in the substrate. Space the plants 1 inch apart. Propagate through cuttings by trimming the stem and replanting it in the soil.
Rapid growth.
Maximum size : 60 cm (24 inch)

Needs

: 73 - 82 °F

CO_2 : optional

: optional

Other varieties
Cabomba Caroliniana
Cabomba Furcata
Cabomba Palaeformis

Soft or tropical Hornwort (*Ceratophyllum submersum*)

 : Background plant

Origin

Type and planting
A stem plant without roots. Refer to the section "Setting up your first aquarium" on page 51 for planting instructions or let it float on the surface. Propagate through cuttings by trimming a lateral shoot to 6 inch.
Rapid growth.
Maximum size : 120 cm (47 inch)

Needs

: 64 - 79 °F

CO_2 : optional

 : optional (and only liquid fertilizer)

Other varieties
Ceratophyllum Demersum

PLANTS SHEETS

Cryptocoryne (Lutea)

: Foreground plant

Origin

Type and planting
A stem plant with roots to be buried in the substrate. Propagate through replanting the stolons produced by the main stem. Rather slow growth.
Maximum size : 20 cm (8 inch)

Needs

: 72 - 82 °F

CO_2 : optional

: recommended

Other varieties
Cryptocoryne Albida
Cryptocoryne crispatula
Cryptocoryne lutea
Cryptocoryne nevillii
Cryptocoryne parva
Cryptocoryne petchii
Cryptocoryne wendtii

Echinodorus (Amazonicus)

: Background plant

Origin

Type and planting
A stem plant with roots to be planted in the soil. Propagate through replanting the stolons produced by the main stem. Moderate growth.
Maximum size : 60 cm (24 inch)

Needs

: 72 - 82 °F

CO_2 : recommended

: recommended

Other varieties
Echinodorus Angustifolius
Echinodorus Aquartica
Echinodorus Beauty red
Echinodorus Bleheri
Echinodorus Bolivianus
Echinodorus Cordifolius ovalis
Echinodorus Latifolius

PLANTS SHEETS

Dwarf baby tears or cuba HC
(*Hemianthus Callitrichoides*)

: Foreground plant

Origin

Type and planting
A delicate carpeting plant with roots to be buried in the substrate. Introduce it into a well-established and balanced aquarium (without algae). Exhibits fairly rapid growth.
Maximum size : 2 cm (1 inch)

Needs
: 64 - 82 °F
CO_2 : recommended
: recommended

Other varieties
Hemianthus Micranthemoides

Hydrocotyle
(Tripartita)

: Foreground plant

Origin

Type and planting
A carpeting plant with roots to be buried in the substrate. Propagate through replanting the stolons produced by the main stem. Rather slow growth rate.
Maximum size : 5 cm (2 inch)

Needs
: 68 - 82 °F
CO_2 : optional
: optional

Other varieties
Hydrocotyle Leucocephala
Hydrocotyle Dissecta
Hydrocotyle Tripartita mini

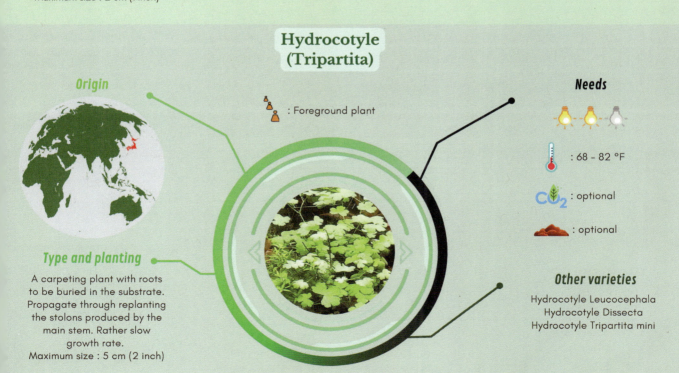

PLANTS SHEETS

Dwarf Hygrophila
(*Hygrophila polysperma*)

Origin

: Background plant

Needs

: 70 – 86 °F

CO_2 : optional

: optional

Type and planting

A stem plant with roots to be buried in the substrate. Space the stems 1 inch apart. Easily propagated by cutting at any level and replanting in the soil. Rapid growth.
Maximum size : 60 cm (24 inch)

Other varieties

Hygrophila Corymbosa
Hygrophila Difformis
Hygrophila Rubela
Hygrophila Salicifolia
Hygrophila Angustifolia
Hygrophila Angustifolia Red

Limnophila
(Heterophylla)

Origin

: Background plant

Needs

: 72 – 82 °F

CO_2 : optional

: recommended (especially for iron)

Type and planting

A stem plant with roots to be buried in the substrate. Space the stems 1 inch apart. Easily propagated by cutting at any level and replanting in the soil. Rapid growth.
Maximum size : 40 cm (16 inch)

Other varieties

Limnophila Sessiliflora
Limnophila Aromatica
Limnophila Scrophulariaceae
Limnophila mini "Vietnam"

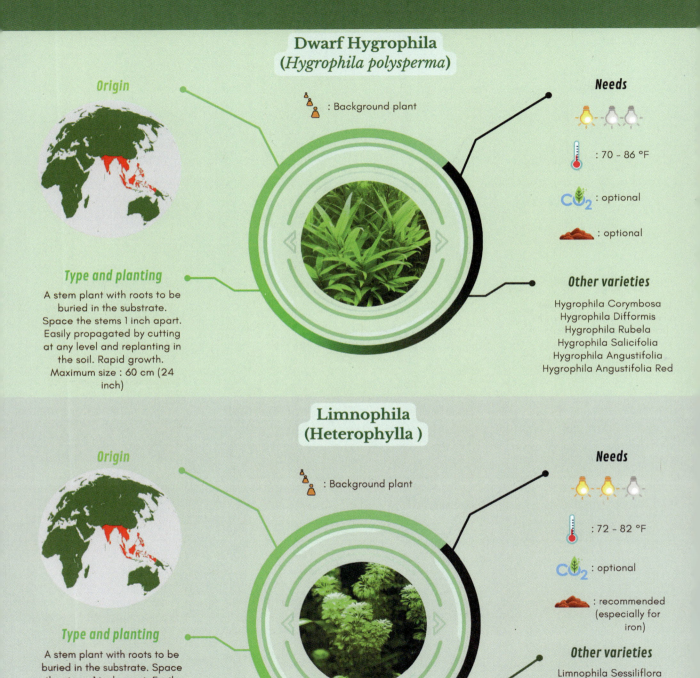

PLANTS SHEETS

Lemna Minor

Origin

: Floating plant

Needs

: 50 – 86 °F

CO_2 : unnecessary

: unnecessary

Type and planting

A highly prolific floating plant that reproduces autonomously, exhibiting a potential doubling of its quantity within a 24-hour timeframe under specific conditions. Characterized by an exceptionally swift growth rate.
Size : 1 cm (0,4 inch)

Other varieties

NA

Cylindric fruit primrose-willow
(*Ludwigia glandulosa*)

Origin

: Median / background plant

Needs

: 68 – 82 °F

CO_2 : required

: required

Type and planting

A plant with stems and roots to be buried in the substrate. Space the plants at a distance of 1 inch each. Easily propagated by cutting the upper portion and replanting it in the soil.
Slow growth pace.
Maximum size : 30 cm (12 inch)

Other varieties

Ludwigia Arcuata
Ludwigia Brevipes
Ludwigia Repens
Ludwigia Dark Red

PLANTS SHEETS

Java Fern
(*Microsorum Pteropus*)

Origin

: Median / background plant

Needs

: 59 – 86 °F

CO_2 : optional

: optional

Type and planting

An epiphytic plant with a rhizome that should be expressly avoided from being buried in the substrate. It is optimal to affix it to a decorative element (such as a root or stone) using either adhesive glue or nylon thread. Slow growth rate.
Maximum size : 40 cm (16 inch)

Other varieties

Microsorum Pteropus trident
Microsorum Pteropus windelov
Microsorum Pteropus mini

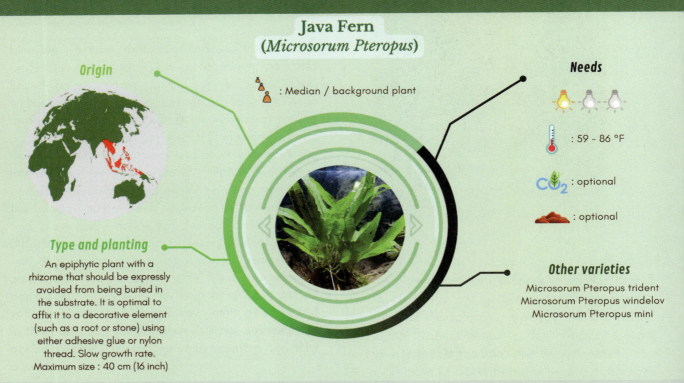

Water Cabbage or Water Lettuce
(*Pistia stratiotes*)

Origin

: Floating plant

Needs

: 61 – 82 °F

CO_2 : optional

: optional

Type and planting

A floating plant, quite prolific given favorable conditions. Requires soft water (GH < 10°) and slightly acidic conditions (pH < 7). Reproduces autonomously through lateral shoots.
Rapid growth.
Maximum size : 30 cm (12 inch)

Other varieties

NA

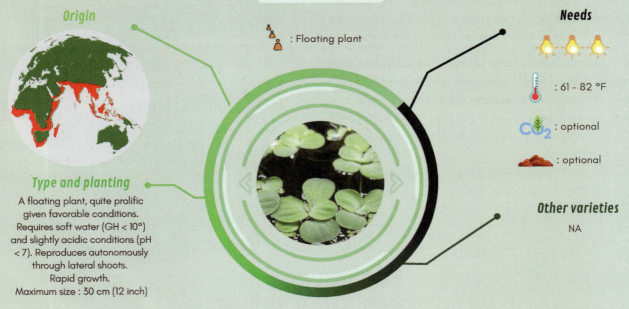

PLANTS SHEETS

Pogostemon (Helferi)

 : Foreground plant

Origin

Type and planting

A diminutive stem plant with roots to be buried in the substrate. Self-expands through the multiplication of lateral shoots.
Adapts gradually, yet subsequently demonstrates a rather brisk growth pace.
Maximum size : 10 cm (4 inch)

Needs

 : 73 - 86 °F

 : optional

 : recommended

Other varieties

Pogostemon Erectus
Pogostemon Octopus

Proserpinaca palustris

 : Background plant

Origin

Type and planting

A plant with roots to be buried in the substrate. The shape and color of the leaves vary depending on the lighting intensity and the water nitrate levels. Achieving its coppery hue requires potent illumination coupled with the lowest possible nitrate levels. Moderately slow growth rate.
Maximum size : 40 cm (16 inch)

Needs

 : 59 - 82 °F

 : required

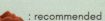 : recommended

Other varieties

NA

PLANTS SHEETS

Dwarf Rotala
(*Rotala Rotundifolia*)

Origin

: Background plant

Needs

: 68 – 86 °F

CO_2 : recommended

: recommended

Type and planting

A stem plant with roots to be buried in the substrate. Maintain a spacing of 1 inch between individual plants. Easily propagated by trimming the stems to approximately 4 inch and replanting them in the soil.
Reasonably brisk growth rate.
Maximum size : 60 cm (24 inch)

Other varieties

Rotala sp. Nanjenshan

Awl-leaf Arrowhead or Dwarf Sagittaria
(*Sagittaria subulata*)

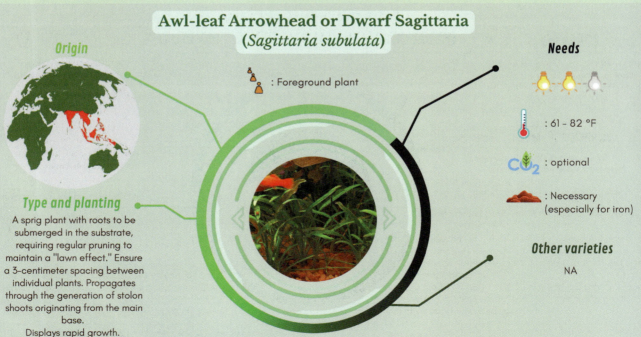

Origin

: Foreground plant

Needs

: 61 – 82 °F

CO_2 : optional

: Necessary (especially for iron)

Type and planting

A sprig plant with roots to be submerged in the substrate, requiring regular pruning to maintain a "lawn effect." Ensure a 3-centimeter spacing between individual plants. Propagates through the generation of stolon shoots originating from the main base.
Displays rapid growth.
Maximum size : 30 cm (12 inch)

Other varieties

NA

PLANTS SHEETS

Java moss or Bogor moss
(*Taxiphyllum Barbieri*)

: Everywhere

Origin

Type and planting
Aquatic moss forming a dense appearance that can be shaped according to preference through pruning. Affix it to a decorative element using a dab of adhesive or nylon thread. Easily multiplies by cutting it into several pieces, each of which will regenerate subsequently.
Reasonably swift growth rate.

Needs

 : 59 - 82 °F
 : optional
 : optional

Other varieties
Taxiphyllum sp. flame Moss
Taxiphyllum sp. spiky

Vallis
(*Vallisneria Gigantea*)

 : Background plant (ideally in front of the filter output)

Origin

Type and planting
A bulbous plant, meant to be partially buried in the soil. Generates stolons from the mother plant that can be detached and replanted once well-developed (at least 2 inch).
Displays rapid growth.
Maximum size : 200 cm (79 inch)

Needs

 : 64 - 82 °F
 : optional
 : required

Other varieties
Vallisneria Spiralis

MOST COMMON DISEASES

FIN ROT

 Symptoms

- Fins exhibiting faded coloration (translucent gray) and/or fraying at the tips.
- Red streaks (blood) may become visible.
- Fins torn into tatters along their entire length in an advanced state.

 Causes

A common disease observed in certain fish, attributed to the morphology of their fins. It may manifest following an injury, such as tearing against a decorative element (sharp decorations, abrasive substrates, etc.). Additionally, it can occur spontaneously due to significant stress, bacterial or viral infections, or fungal issues (related to maintenance problems).

 Fin rot is more prevalent among fish with long, flowing fins, such as goldfish, bettas, guppies, mollies, and others.

 Curability

The ease of treatment varies depending on the progression of the rot. It becomes more challenging when the decay is located on the dorsal fin or has reached the body, nearly incurable and fatal in such instances.

 Treatment

1st method : With antibacterial product
Best performed in a hospital tank

- Isolate the fish in a hospital tank with a capacity of 0,5 to 1 gallon
- Place only a small heater set at 75°F.
- Use an antibacterial and following the recommendations in the instructions.

2nd method : Salt bath (with low concentration)
To be carried out in a hospital tank

- Isolate the fish in a hospital tank with a capacity of 2 to 5 liters
- Place only a small heater set between 75°F and 79°F.
- Dissolve a teaspoon of Guérande salt (~25g) per gallon of water and a cattapa leaf

Change the water every 1 to 2 days with water with the same parameters (temperature, salt concentration, etc.). The treatment is to be carried out until the regrowth of the fins (transparent parts at the end).

WHITE SPOT OR ICH
(ICHTHYOPHTHIRIUS MULTIFILIIS)

 Symptoms

- Fins clamped against the body.
- Erratic swimming, with the fish rubbing against decorations.
- Presence of white spots approximately 0.5 mm in size on the fins and body in an advanced stage.

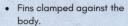 **Causes**

The white spots are attributed to a parasite known as Ichthyophthirius multifiliis. Highly contagious, its development occurs in two alternating phases :

- The free-swimming phase, during which the parasite reproduces outside the fish, in the aquarium water.
- The infection phase, wherein it colonizes its host.

 Livebearers (especially Molly and Xipho), Botias, and Metynnis are particularly susceptible to this parasitic condition.

 Curability

The white spot disease is generally treatable, provided one responds promptly and isolates the affected fish to prevent its spread.

Treatment

1st method : with antibacterial
To be carried out ideally in a hospital tank

- Heat the tank above 84°F
- Use an antibacterial and follow the instructions

2nd method : with salt bath (high concentration)
To be carried out in a hospital tank

- Heating water above 84°F and add 100 grams of salt per gallon of water
- Then put the fish in it (after having acclimatized it to the temperature
- Leave it for 15 minutes and desalinate gradually : replace 1/3 of the water with new water. Then 50% after one to two hours. Finally, another 50% an hour later.

In case of abnormal behavior during the bath (hazardous swimming, on the back, ...), it will be imperative to desalinate immediately and remove the fish.

MOST COMMON DISEASES

VELVET (*OODINIUM PILLULARIS*)

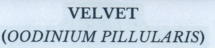

Symptoms

- Dull and less flexible colors in both fins and body (appearing stuck together).
- Loss of appetite.
- Rapid breathing.
- White/yellowish spots on the skin and fins, resembling the fish has been covered in a golden powder.
- Rubbing against decorations.

Causes

Velvet is caused by a parasite that attaches itself and develops on the scales and gills of the fish. Highly contagious, it can be initially mistaken for white spot disease. Without a host, the parasite cannot survive for more than 6 days.

 The parasite responsible for velvet (belonging to the dinoflagellate family) is highly contagious. Disinfect the tank using a UV sterilizer or wait for 6 days without fish in the aquarium to ensure the parasite's demise.

Curability

Oodinium is generally treatable, provided one reacts promptly and isolates the affected fish to prevent its spread.

Treatment

1st method : with antibacteriale
To be carried out absolutely in a hospital tank

- Place the hospital tank heated to 84°F in the dark
- Use an antibacterial and follow the instructions

2nd method : with salt bath (high concentration)
To be carried out in a hospital tank, invertebrates and plants are not tolerant of salt

Same procedure as for the treatment of white spot disease (page 130)

Consider treating the entire tank to eliminate parasites and their spores before reintroducing any fish into it.

FUNGAL INFECTION

Symptoms

- Loss of appetite.
- Decoloration.
- Apathy.
- Cottony white patches and/or tufts on the body and head.

Causes

Infection often caused by poor maintenance, particularly with a low temperature that promotes the attack of naturally occurring fungal spores in the water.

 Poor maintenance coupled with an injury to the fish's mucus layer promotes this disease. Exercise caution during fish handling, especially with a net, as it can be a source of such injuries.

Curability

Easily treatable, but it is imperative to administer treatment promptly. Otherwise, it can be fatal.

Treatment

With antibacteriale
To be carried out ideally in a hospital tank

- Heat the tank between 77 and 81°F
- Use an antifungal products and follow the instructions

A nearly complete water change and a preventive treatment of the tank are necessary to prevent the contamination of other inhabitants.

MOST COMMON DISEASES

ACIDOSIS - ALKALOSIS

Symptoms
- Discoloration (browning in the case of discus).
- Respiratory difficulties (fish gasping for air at the surface).
- Loss of appetite.
- Erratic swimming or immobility near the surface.
- Excessive mucus secretion.
- Possible formation of ulcers.

Causes
Sudden decrease in pH leading to acidosis (resulting, for instance, from uncontrolled CO_2 injection or biogenic decalcification), or conversely, an increase for alkalosis (rarer), possibly stemming from the dissolution of limestone rocks.

Curability
Fatal if the response is too delayed. Monitor the condition of the fish closely even after the issue is corrected. Acidosis/alkalosis significantly weakens the immune system.

Treatment
Involves correcting water parameters (pH and KH)

- Initiate a gradual water change with water rich in bicarbonates (KH above 6) to buffer the pH.

- Replace 30 to 40% with an immediate water change, then an additional 20% if necessary, to restore an acceptable pH level (between 6 and 7.5).

> *i* In discus fish, acidosis/alkalosis often affects the gills, causing them to turn brownish, and results in excessive mucus secretion.

HYDROPISIA

Symptoms
- Abdominal swelling.
- Loss of appetite.
- Mucous excrement in the form of white filaments.
- Raised scales, giving the appearance of a "pinecone."
- Bulging eyes.

Causes
Hydropsy is not a disease per se but a general weakening of the fish leading to various complications. It can be caused by several factors, independent or cumulative: poor maintenance, viral or bacterial infection, intense stress, bad food, etc. The intestine is often the first affected organ. The intestinal mucosa breaks down and is expelled in excrement (form of white filaments). It becomes permeable, allowing pathogens to enter, leading to a cascade of complications such as liver or kidney necrosis, subsequently causing renal failure. In the final stage, internal fluids, unable to be eliminated, accumulate in abdominal cavities (swollen abdomen), scale pockets (raised scales), or behind the eyes (bulging eyes).

Curability
Hydropsy is often fatal as the symptoms become noticeable in the advanced stages of the disease. Euthanasia is often the most humane course of action to consider, preventing further suffering for the fish.

Treatment
A last chance treatment can be attempted, but its success rate remains relatively very low.

The procedure :
- Isolate the fish in a hospital tank
- Place only a small heater set between 88 and 90°F
Many bacteria are much less active at these temperatures
- Dissolve a teaspoon of salt (~25g) per gallon of water (low concentration) and half a cattapa leaf
- Use a strong antibacterial and follow the instructions
- Place the tray in total darkness and apply the treatment for 3/4 days.

MOST COMMON DISEASES

OXYGEN DEFICIT

Symptoms

- Fish cluster at the water surface, gulping air.
- Rapid and erratic breathing.

Curability

Fatal through suffocation if the response is too delayed. Monitor the condition of the fish closely even after correcting the issue. Oxygen deficiency, even if brief, can significantly weaken the immune system.

Causes

Poor maintenance leading to excessive water pollution (overcrowding, overfeeding, plant decay). The increased activity of denitrifying bacteria depletes the water's oxygen levels (as they also consume oxygen). Simultaneously, nitrites hinder the attachment of oxygen to the fish's red blood cells.
This can also result from poor gas exchange between oxygen and carbon dioxide: inadequate filtration circulation, excessive CO2 diffusion, high temperature, etc.

Treatment

Check the water parameters and the setup

- Test for nitrite levels (potentially ammonia and nitrates as well).
- Monitor the CO2 levels in the water (using tests or checking pH and KH values).
- Verify the proper flow of the filter and the direction of discharge (towards the surface or slightly below the water level).
- Consider adding an air stone to enhance water oxygenation, especially in the case of elevated temperatures.

 An oxygen deficit is more likely to occur during the summer, when the water temperature rises.

You now have all the information to embark on this incredible journey into the world of aquarium keeping. We wish you much joy and many enjoyable hours observing your aquatic realm and its inhabitants.

If this guide has been helpful, please feel free to let us know by leaving a comment in the space below.

Discover our other publications dedicated to the world of aquarium keeping :

See you soon.

© AquaHealth